T0054109

THE MEDITERRANEAN DASH DIET COOKBOOK

THE Mediterranean DASH DIET

COOKBOOK

LOWER YOUR BLOOD PRESSURE AND IMPROVE YOUR HEALTH

ABBIE GELLMAN, MS, RD, CDN

ROCKRIDGE
PRESS

Copyright © 2019 by Rockridge Press, Emeryville, California

No part of this publication may be reproduced, stored in a retrieval system or transmitted in any form or by any means, electronic, mechanical, photocopying, recording, scanning or otherwise, except as permitted under Sections 107 or 108 of the 1976 United States Copyright Act, without the prior written permission of the Publisher. Requests to the Publisher for permission should be addressed to the Permissions Department, Rockridge Press, 6005 Shellmound Street, Suite 175, Emeryville, CA 94608.

Limit of Liability/Disclaimer of Warranty: The Publisher and the author make no representations or warranties with respect to the accuracy or completeness of the contents of this work and specifically disclaim all warranties, including without limitation warranties of fitness for a particular purpose. No warranty may be created or extended by sales or promotional materials. The advice and strategies contained herein may not be suitable for every situation. This work is sold with the understanding that the Publisher is not engaged in rendering medical, legal, or other professional advice or services. If professional assistance is required, the services of a competent professional person should be sought. Neither the Publisher nor the author shall be liable for damages arising herefrom. The fact that an individual, organization or website is referred to in this work as a citation and/or potential source of further information does not mean that the author or the Publisher endorses the information the individual, organization or website may provide or recommendations they/it may make. Further, readers should be aware that Internet websites listed in this work may have changed or disappeared between when this work was written and when it is read.

For general information on our other products and services or to obtain technical support, please contact our Customer Care Department within the U.S. at (866) 744-2665, or outside the U.S. at (510) 253-0500.

Rockridge Press publishes its books in a variety of electronic and print formats. Some content that appears in print may not be available in electronic books, and vice versa.

TRADEMARKS: Rockridge Press and the Rockridge Press logo are trademarks or registered trademarks of Callisto Media Inc. and/or its affiliates, in the United States and other countries, and may not be used without written permission. All other trademarks are the property of their respective owners. Rockridge Press is not associated with any product or vendor mentioned in this book.

Art Producer: Sara Feinstein
Editor: Bridget Fitzgerald
Production Editor: Kayla Park
Production Manager: Martin Worthington
Photography: Photography © Moya McAllister, cover, p.ii-iii, vi, x, 24, 40, 62, 82, 104, 124, 142, 157; Nadine Greef, p. v. Author photo courtesy of © DooDad Studios, Pacific Coast Producers.
Food styling by Sean Dooley, cover, p.ii-iii, vi, x, 24, 40, 62, 82, 104, 124, 142, 157.

ISBN: Print 978-1-64152-793-4 | eBook 978-1-64152-794-1

RO

For Olivia—
my mini-me, the other Gellman Girl,
the reason I took a chance on me,
and a constant reminder that doing
what I love every day is possible.

Contents

Introduction

Food has many meanings and represents different things to different people. At its most literal, food is nourishment; it is fuel for our bodies and nature's medicine. Food is also pleasure and joy. No one role is more important than the other, and it is these basic ideas that I strive to remember when creating recipes and feeding myself and others.

As both a chef and a registered dietitian, my passion and overall goal is to help people cook and eat more healthily. The Mediterranean DASH diet, a style of eating and cooking I have followed for years, makes this very simple. This diet doesn't involve a ton of rules, and it never sacrifices flavor or nutrients. It features straightforward recipes, often rich in beans, vegetables, lean protein, whole grains, herbs, and spices—and it's these recipes that empower the viewers and readers of my videos and website, CulinaryNutritionCuisine.com.

The DASH (Dietary Approaches to Stop Hypertension) diet is designed to help you lower your blood pressure, improve cardiac health, reduce the risk of cancer and type 2 diabetes, and, in some cases, lose weight. The Mediterranean diet is based on a pattern of eating, cooking, and other lifestyle factors that focuses on an abundance of whole foods. These two diets overlap in many areas, but merging them fully creates a powerful duo that is sustainable—and delicious—for the long term. It's no wonder they've been the top two diets, as ranked by *U.S. News & World Report*, for many years running.

Combining the two diets creates a unique approach to the DASH diet that is incredibly flexible, full of vegetarian and pescatarian options, and makes cooking at home or eating out easy and achievable. Once you get the hang of the basics and begin to build up your recipe arsenal, tweaking your favorite dishes will become second nature. You will never have to fear running out of recipe ideas again!

As someone who has a deep love for both food and health, I've filled this book with satisfying dishes rooted in the flavorful culinary traditions of Greece, Italy, and Spain, among others, and included tips to make committing to this nutritionally balanced way of eating as easy as possible. I hope you'll find the information in this book and the recipes as useful and tasty as I do. Here are some things you can expect to find as you make your way through this book.

- Guidelines for following the DASH diet and Mediterranean lifestyle diet, plus the specific health benefits of each

- Easy, delicious recipes that adhere to both diets

- Healthy ingredients easily found at your local grocery store

- Recipes that focus on whole, minimally processed foods

- Dishes you can enjoy even if you have allergy or dietary requirements, including recipes that are gluten-free, dairy-free, nut-free, or vegan

- Substitution Tips and Ingredient Tips that provide helpful information, shortcuts, and food swaps based on ingredient availability or food preferences

- Nutrition information for each recipe

Thanks for joining me in the kitchen! I hope you love the Mediterranean DASH diet as much as I do!

CHAPTER 1

The Best Diet Isn't a Diet

"Diet" can be a dirty word to some people, but it doesn't have to be. A diet is simply a way of eating. Eating is a vital part of life—ideally a pleasurable and healthy part of life—and not a trendy fad. The DASH diet is a flexible, balanced way of eating that helps create a healthy routine in your daily life. The Mediterranean diet approach should be viewed as a lifestyle, focusing on flavor, texture, and the simple joy of eating. The focus is on whole foods, mostly plants, prepared in a manner designed to maintain a food's nutritional integrity, so health and wellness benefits naturally follow. The Mediterranean DASH diet is my favorite approach to an overall healthy lifestyle—and the very best "forever diet."

WHAT IS THE DASH DIET?

Just hearing the words "DASH diet," if you've never heard them before, may invoke visions of fast food or grab-and-go fare, but this style of eating is anything but that. An acronym for Dietary Approaches to Stop Hypertension, the DASH diet was created as a method to help lower blood pressure, although you can most certainly benefit from this style of eating even if your blood pressure isn't a concern. The goal of decreased blood pressure is achieved by consuming whole foods and focusing on an eating pattern that is rich in potassium, magnesium, and calcium, with moderate levels of sodium.

The DASH diet has been around for more than two decades and was ranked the number 1 best diet overall by *US News and World Report* for eight consecutive years, only dropping to number 2—behind the Mediterranean diet—for the first time in 2019. The National Institutes of Health (NIH) National Heart, Lung, and Blood Institute (NHLBI) has funded five studies examining the DASH diet's health benefits. Researchers found that it can lower both blood pressure and LDL cholesterol, also known as the "bad cholesterol." When compared to a standard American diet, the DASH diet has been shown to help with weight loss, cardiovascular health, and lowering the risk of type 2 diabetes. In addition to helping in many areas related to hypertension and disease risk factors, it is a way of eating that promotes overall wellness and fosters a healthy lifestyle.

Why Mediterranean?

The idea of a Mediterranean diet and lifestyle is not a new one. It is based on a way of cooking, eating, and general lifestyle practices found in countries that surround the Mediterranean Sea, including Greece, Turkey, Spain, Italy, Israel, Croatia, and Egypt. While the exact cuisine found in each country may differ, the underlying themes are the same.

Similar to DASH, the Mediterranean diet is a plant-based approach to eating that focuses on an abundance of whole foods, such as fruit, vegetables, nuts, legumes, and whole grains. Fish, shellfish, and low-fat dairy are the preferred protein sources, and lean proteins in the form of eggs, meat, and poultry are absolutely fine in smaller portions. There is an emphasis on incorporating healthy fats, with olive oil as the recommended staple. Other foods containing healthy fats are highlighted, such as avocados, nuts, and seeds. The Mediterranean diet also limits sweets and sodium and relies heavily on the use of herbs and spices for flavor. Water is the preferred beverage, but red wine in moderation is allowed and encouraged with meals.

In addition to specific foods, there are other important factors to the Mediterranean lifestyle, including daily physical activity and making meals into social occasions with family and friends.

Why It Works

Hundreds of scientific studies have linked the Mediterranean and DASH diets to decreased risk of cardiovascular disease, cancer, type 2 diabetes, and dementia, to name only a few. According to a study published in the *American Journal of Medicine*, the Mediterranean diet beat low-fat diets for weight loss and improved heart health after one year. In addition, a study in the *Journal of the American Medical Association* of about 26,000 women found that those following the Mediterranean diet had up to a 28 percent lower risk of heart disease, likely due to the diet's ability to help reduce body mass index (BMI), improve insulin function, and decrease inflammation.

Following are some key principles of the Mediterranean DASH diet and the benefits provided:

HIGH FIBER

At least 25 grams of fiber daily is recommended. A diet rich in fiber helps reduce inflammation by promoting movement through your digestive system, adding bulk to your stool, and lowering cholesterol levels. Fiber is naturally occurring in whole grains, fruits, vegetables, and other whole foods. Research from the Federation of American Societies for Experimental Biology (FASEB) has found a link between fewer indications of systemic inflammation and higher fiber intake. In other words, the more, the better!

THE RIGHT FATS

Saturated fats, which should be minimal, are primarily found in animal products; however, they are also found in tropical plant sources such as coconut oil. Studies have shown that regular consumption of saturated fats promotes inflammation, particularly in

 ## Favorite Flavors

Mediterranean recipes are known for their simple cooking techniques and use of fresh, often local, whole foods, such as tomatoes, peppers, garlic, onions, olives, and citrus. The Mediterranean diet is also naturally low in sodium, drawing on flavor from fresh herbs and spices like parsley, basil, oregano, chives, mint, rosemary, thyme, bay leaves, sumac, and za'atar. Other staple ingredients, including cheese, yogurt, tahini, wine, olive oil, vinegars, and harissa, also add wonderful flavor. If I had to describe my perfect meal, it would be fresh-caught branzino prepared with tomatoes, olives, and feta cheese, accompanied by a glass of red wine!

fat tissue, and can contribute to heart disease. Limit saturated fats by choosing lean animal protein sources, such as seafood, lean cuts of meat and poultry, eggs, and low-fat dairy.

Focus instead on unsaturated fats, which are found primarily in vegetables, nuts, and seeds, such as olives, walnuts, and sesame seeds. A study in the *American Journal of Clinical Nutrition* found that people who ate three servings of nuts on a weekly basis had lower indications of inflammation.

MORE OMEGA-3 FATTY ACIDS

Research shows that omega-3 fatty acids, found in foods like walnuts and fatty fish, can help reduce inflammation and may help lower the risk of chronic diseases such as heart disease, cancer, and arthritis. The Mediterranean DASH diet is full of foods high in omega-3 fatty acids.

NO PROCESSED FOODS

Processed foods are often refined sugars and refined carbohydrates that generally contain excessive fat, sugar, and/or salt. This includes any food that contains high fructose corn syrup or excessive sodium, both of which contribute to inflammation throughout the body.

SHARED BENEFITS

With an emphasis on natural, nutrient-dense foods, both the DASH and Mediterranean diets help to prevent the onset of chronic disease and promote longevity. They are not fad diets or trends that promise drastic short-term results, but are rooted in a solid foundation based on long-term health and lifestyle goals.

Lower Blood Pressure

Enjoying a healthy diet full of foods rich in potassium, calcium, and magnesium, while consuming less sodium, has been found to be an effective way to help lower blood pressure. The Mediterranean DASH diet is full of these minerals (and more) due to the abundance of whole fruits, vegetables, and dairy, to name a few.

Improved Heart Health

The Mediterranean DASH diet strongly emphasizes healthy fats, including nuts, seeds, and olive oil, which have been shown to be beneficial for heart health in general, but also in the prevention of cardiovascular disease. Following this diet pattern also provides significant dietary fiber, which further supports healthy cholesterol levels as well as lowering the risk of heart disease, stroke, and obesity.

Diabetes Prevention

Plant-based diets, like the Mediterranean DASH diet, are a major contributor to our daily fiber intake. The fiber found in plant foods, including fruits, vegetables, nuts, legumes, and whole grains, helps to slow the absorption of glucose in the blood, making it an essential tool in the prevention and management of diabetes.

Weight Loss

Both the Mediterranean and DASH diets emphasize consuming whole foods, including fruits, vegetables, whole grains, lean protein, and healthy fats. This style of eating naturally lends itself to choosing fewer processed foods, a lower caloric intake, a higher quality of foods, and may lead to weight loss. A 2016 study by the

American Journal of Clinical Nutrition showed that people following a Mediterranean diet, in particular those who regularly included olive oil, lost the most weight.

Improved Digestion

The foods we eat can foster the growth of a healthy, or unhealthy, gut environment. The focus on whole, unprocessed foods in the Mediterranean DASH diet promotes the proliferation of beneficial gut bacteria, which helps to decrease inflammation and supports a stable, healthy, and happy gut microbiome.

Reduced Cancer Risk

The Mediterranean and DASH diets are rich in antioxidants and anti-inflammatory foods, all of which help to lower the risk of cancer. Studies have shown that a Mediterranean dietary pattern has an inverse relationship associated with lower rates of several types of cancer.

Better Sleep

A study published in the journal *Clinical Nutrition ESPEN* found that adherence to the Mediterranean diet improved overall sleep quality, particularly for those between 65 and 75 years of age. The DASH diet is rich in magnesium, which supports a number of functions in the body, one in particular being better sleep quality. Magnesium can be found in foods such as dark leafy greens, nuts and seeds, legumes, and dairy products.

The Mediterranean DASH diet is a relatively simple eating plan. The focus is on whole foods with some general guidelines regarding specific food groups. Our attention is placed on fruits, vegetables, whole grains, healthy fats, lean protein, and legumes. Emphasis on these foods helps to naturally decrease overall consumption of saturated fat, refined sugar, and sodium. So how do we do this?

Whole Grains and Starchy Vegetables

Whole grains and starchy vegetables are good sources of fiber, helping to slow the absorption of glucose in the blood. Packed with vitamins and minerals, these foods should always be chosen over refined and processed carbohydrates. Whole grains include brown rice, barley, farro, quinoa, oats, and whole-grain pasta; starchy vegetables include potatoes and sweet potatoes.

Servings: Aim for four to six servings daily. One serving equates to one-half cup of cooked grains, one slice of whole grain bread, or one medium-size sweet potato.

Helpful Tips and Tricks: Short on time or don't want to cook? No problem! Instead of making a pot of brown rice, you can look for precooked, frozen whole grains in your grocer's freezer aisle.

Fruits and Vegetables

Fruits and vegetables are a vital part of the Mediterranean DASH diet. Full of vitamins, minerals, and antioxidants, these are nutrient powerhouses in our day-to-day life. These fiber-rich foods help us feel full and satisfied, support lower blood pressure and weight management, and help ward off a variety of diseases. Be sure to eat plenty of alliums, such as garlic, onions, and leeks, as well as a good amount of crucifers, including broccoli, cauliflower, and Brussels sprouts, on a weekly basis.

Servings: Aim to consume at least four to five servings of vegetables and three servings of fruit daily. One serving equates to one-half cup of fruit or cooked vegetables, or one cup of raw leafy greens.

Helpful Tips and Tricks: Fresh and frozen will be your go-to foundation, but canned and packed in water or natural juices are great to keep on hand as a backup option. And don't forget dried fruit, a great addition to your yogurt or oatmeal or sprinkled on top of a salad!

 Building a Plate

Traditional Mediterranean cuisine is enjoyed as part of a balanced lifestyle, which includes a sustainable approach to eating well. The cornerstone of any healthy diet is a properly proportioned plate. Fruits and vegetables are eaten in plenty, while meats, sweet treats, and wine are enjoyed in moderation. A balanced plate should be one-half non-starchy vegetables, one-quarter whole grains or starchy vegetables, and one-quarter lean protein.

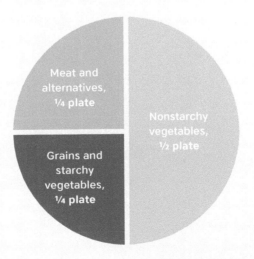

Meat and alternatives, ¼ plate

Nonstarchy vegetables, ½ plate

Grains and starchy vegetables, ¼ plate

Lean Proteins: Animal and Plant

Lean proteins encompass both animal and plant-based protein sources. In the Mediterranean DASH diet, we place a heavier emphasis on fish and shellfish, with smaller portions of eggs, lean poultry, and meat. When selecting beef, pork, and other animal protein, look for leaner cuts, such as loin and round. These cuts of meat are flavorful and easy to prepare while also being lower in saturated fat. Eggs and poultry are largely excellent choices as well.

Plant-based protein sources are superstars. They are high in fiber and complex carbohydrates while being low in fat. They are also sources of other key minerals and nutrients, such as potassium, magnesium, folate, and iron. Plant-based proteins include beans and legumes, such as lentils, peas, and soy. For our purposes, nuts and seeds will also be part of this category, contributing lean protein and healthy fats.

Servings: Aim to get up to six ounces per day of lean meat, poultry, or seafood. Think of a three-ounce portion as the size of a deck of playing cards. Try to get two to three servings of seafood on a weekly basis. Aim for four to five servings of nuts, seeds, beans, and legumes per week. One serving is about one-half cup cooked beans or legumes, three ounces of tempeh or tofu, and one-third cup of nuts and seeds.

Helpful Tips and Tricks: Keep low-sodium versions of canned tuna, salmon, and beans on hand to help get meals on the table quickly and easily.

Healthy Fats and Oils

Olives and olive oil are staples in the Mediterranean DASH diet, known for their heart-healthy monounsaturated fat content and anti-inflammatory properties. For a more neutral-flavored oil, canola oil is a good choice.

Another great source of healthy fat is the avocado. Research has shown that the high levels of oleic acid found in avocados help decrease LDL, the "bad" cholesterol, and boost HDL, the "good" cholesterol.

Servings: Aim for two to three servings of fats and oils daily. One serving equates to one teaspoon of oil or one-quarter of an avocado.

Helpful Tips and Tricks: Making your own salad dressing is a great way to incorporate flavorful, low-sodium versions into your daily routine. Use empty jam or nut butter jars to make larger batches, which will keep in the refrigerator for a couple of weeks.

Low-Fat Dairy

Low-fat dairy foods such as cheese and yogurt are foundational foods in the Mediterranean DASH diet. The dairy group contributes important nutrients, including calcium, vitamin D, and potassium. Studies have shown that fermented dairy products, such as yogurt and some cheeses, have an inverse relationship with cardiovascular disease and type 2 diabetes. There is some evidence that eating *fermented* dairy foods may help fight inflammation associated with the development of heart disease.

Servings: Aim to consume two to three servings of low-fat dairy daily. One serving equates to one cup of nonfat or low-fat plain yogurt (includes Greek yogurt) or one-and-a-half ounces of cheese.

Helpful Tips and Tricks: Have a hankering for tuna salad? Use plain yogurt in place of mayonnaise to add protein, flavor, and richness without the added saturated fat and calories. Yogurt can also be added to foods like soup and oatmeal to increase the protein content and add creaminess without using butter or heavy cream.

Limited Added Sugar

The Mediterranean DASH diet naturally decreases sugar intake without making you feel deprived in any way. Dessert and sweet treats can still be part of your weekly routine, but with a focus on natural sources of sugar, such as fruit sugars, honey, and maple syrup.

Servings: Aim to limit sugar to five or fewer servings per week. One serving size equals one tablespoon of maple syrup or honey, or one-half cup of ice cream or frozen yogurt.

Helpful Tips and Tricks: Try adding fresh or dried fruit and a teaspoon of jam to a bowl of oatmeal or yogurt in place of sugar.

Limited Sodium

Many foods naturally contain some sodium. However, much of the sodium many of us consume is added to foods, making it too easy for most people to overconsume. You can find it hiding in most processed foods and often added in huge quantities to restaurant meals. Excessive sodium intake is one of the main drivers of high blood pressure. Using less salt, and instead relying on herbs and spices to add bold flavor to foods, is a key component of the Mediterranean DASH diet.

Servings: Aim to consume between 1,500 and 2,300 milligrams of sodium per day. For reference, one-quarter teaspoon of kosher salt equals about 500 milligrams of sodium.

Helpful Tips and Tricks: Reach for herbs and spices to create depth of flavor, adding salt in small amounts. You can always add salt, but once it's there you cannot take it away!

The recipes included in the Mediterranean DASH diet follow these guidelines:

Snacks, sides, and desserts: ≤ 300 milligrams of sodium

Entrées and meals: ≤ 570 milligrams of sodium

To keep your sodium intake in check, it is essential to be able to properly read a food label. The first step is to become familiar with portion sizing (i.e., if you eat two servings worth of a food, you double your sodium intake). As with sugar, it is important to recognize the difference between naturally occurring sodium in foods and added salt. Some foods, like celery, beets, and milk, organically contain sodium in low levels, which supply our bodies with electrolytes. Added salt is salt added during cooking and processing, and this is what accounts for most of our daily sodium intake. Examples of foods typically loaded with added salt include canned foods, cured and deli-style meats, cheeses, frozen prepared meals, soups, chips, and condiments. To help prevent excessive sodium intake, look for foods labeled "no salt added," "low-sodium," or "sodium-free." When using canned items, such as beans and lentils, rinse well with water prior to using. And try using garlic, citrus juice, herbs, and spices for flavor before reaching for the saltshaker.

Nutrition Facts

8 servings per container

Serving size   **1/2 Cup (120mL)**

Amount Per Serving

Calories   160

	% Daily Value*
Total Fat 18g	23%
Saturated Fat 10g	50%
Trans Fat 0g	
Cholesterol 0mg	0%
Sodium 0mg	0%
Total Carbohydrate 0g	0%
Dietary Fiber 0g	0%
Total Sugars 0g	
Includes 0g Added Sugars	0%
Protein 0g	0%

Not a significant source of vitamin D, calcium, iron, and potassium

*The % Daily Value (DV) tells you how much a nutrient in a serving of food contributes to a daily diet. 2,000 calories a day is used for general nutrition advice.

 **Snacking**

Unlike the heavily processed "snack foods" that line the shelves of American supermarkets, snacks common to the Mediterranean DASH diet consist of fresh, whole foods like nuts, seeds, fruit, vegetables, yogurt, and hummus. When cravings hit, opt for these foods in balanced portions. For example, one cup of plain yogurt with one-quarter cup fruit, one cup raw vegetables with one-quarter cup hummus, or an apple with one-quarter cup nuts instead of reaching for packaged foods. See pages 50, 59, and 61 for more ideas.

THE MEDITERRANEAN DASH KITCHEN

Getting your Mediterranean DASH kitchen and pantry together does not require a lot of expensive or difficult-to-find ingredients. Many of the essentials are likely to be in your home already.

The easiest way to get started is to take a look at your pantry, refrigerator, and freezer and get rid of things that will keep you from meeting your goals (see Foods to Swap, page 16). Then stock up on the Foods to Reach For, below, so you always have healthy essentials on hand.

Foods to Reach For

These will be the staples of your diet, what you'll use again and again. You do not need to purchase everything on this list but try to select some items from each category to have available. For example, keep a few cans of beans, a bag of dried lentils, canned tuna, and quinoa in the pantry. This list can also be helpful to steer you in the right direction when eating at a restaurant or away from home.

Whole grains: brown rice, quinoa, oats, farro, etc.

Whole fruits: fresh, frozen, jarred, canned in water, and dried (no sugar added)

Whole vegetables: fresh, frozen, jarred, and canned

Beans and legumes: canned and dried

Fish and seafood: fresh, frozen, and canned

Low-fat dairy: plain yogurt, milk, cheese, and cottage cheese

Nuts and seeds: walnuts, pistachios, chia seeds, pumpkin seeds, etc. (unsalted when possible)

Vegetable oils: especially olive oil, avocado oil, and canola oil

Vinegar: balsamic, red wine vinegar, white wine vinegar, etc.

 ## Mediterranean Spices

Most Mediterranean spices are things you have tried before and are familiar with, including garlic, basil, and parsley. However, there are three spices I love and have included in some of the recipes that may be new to you: sumac, za'atar, and harissa. Sumac is a dried ground spice that is dark red and has a citrusy flavor. If you cannot find it in your local grocery store, you can order it online or simply use citrus zest instead. Za'atar is a spice mixture typically composed of sesame seeds, thyme, and sumac. You can easily make your own za'atar spice blend if you like. Harissa is a Mediterranean chili paste and is most commonly found ready-made in jars and tubes.

Foods to Moderate

These are foods to include in your daily or weekly routine, but should be consumed in moderation.

Kosher salt or sea salt: A primary focus of the DASH diet is decreasing sodium levels. Much of our sodium intake can be found in the form of processed foods, including frozen dinners and packaged snacks like chips and crackers. When buying canned foods, look for "low-sodium" or "no salt" labels. Overall, aim for three-quarters to one teaspoon maximum per day, or 1,500 to 2,300 milligrams.

Added sugar: Sometimes adding sugar to a dish is essential, but look to more nutritious sources of sweetness, such as honey and maple syrup. These choices add depth of flavor and some nutritional benefits, such as zinc, manganese, and antioxidants. Limit to five servings per week.

Wine: The Mediterranean DASH diet lifestyle includes making meals social occasions. Savoring food among family and friends can include enjoying the occasional glass of wine.

Foods to Swap

Whenever possible, try to avoid these items and instead swap them out with alternatives. The Mediterranean DASH diet recipes are a great place to start making the switch to healthier choices. For example, keeping a batch of Roasted Red Pepper Hummus (page 50) or Baked Eggplant Baba Ganoush (page 51) on hand with some cut up vegetables makes a great go-to snack. Don't want to cook but craving something savory or crunchy? Try a piece of cheese or grab a handful of nuts. Have a hankering for something sweet? Turn to a bowl of fresh fruit with low-fat plain yogurt or some dried fruit.

Processed foods: These are refined sugars and refined carbohydrates that generally contain excessive fat, sugar, and/or salt. Examples include fast food, frozen meals, packaged crackers and chips, and prepackaged baked goods and desserts.

Beverages with empty calories: These are drinks that have a considerable amount of sugar, including soda, sweet tea, sports drinks, and energy drinks. Opt for water or plain tea instead and try to avoid drinking your calories.

A FOREVER LIFESTYLE

We can achieve health and wellness with a long-term view of eating, moving, and living.

Think about the Mediterranean DASH diet as a way of life; it is an easy, realistic way to eat that can be followed long term. Fiber-filled fruits and vegetables, healthy fats, and lean protein will keep you feeling full and satisfied, regular physical activity will keep you energized, and adequate sleep will keep you alert and active, all of which supports a healthy mind and body.

Food Habits

Following the Mediterranean DASH diet and lifestyle does not require drastic changes overnight. Think about your long-term goals and start small with simple, manageable changes that work for you. Try:

- adding a vegetable or fruit to every meal

- going vegan for a meal or two every week

- snacking on a handful of nuts instead of chips and crackers

- filling at least half your plate with plant-based foods

- experimenting with herbs and spices

- having fruit for dessert

- eating seasonally and locally, especially if you have access to a farmers' market

- slowing down and savoring your food and the people around you

Exercise

One of my favorite sayings is "assume the vertical," or, in other words, get up! Physical movement is crucial for optimal health and wellness and is a staple of the Mediterranean lifestyle. All physical movement counts, from going for a walk to climbing stairs to doing yoga. You don't need to train for a marathon or take strenuous spinning classes. Instead, work toward consistency and aim for at least an hour of activity five days a week. If you are someone who sits quite a bit due to work and life factors, think about standing up for 5 to 10 minutes every 45 minutes that you are sitting. Looking for more reasons to exercise? How about these:

- Exercise combats disease

- Exercise reduces chronic pain

- Exercise helps control weight

- Exercise improves mood

- Exercise improves energy

- Exercise boosts sex drive

- Exercise promotes better sleep

Whatever exercise you choose, the bottom line is that staying as active as you can throughout the week supports a healthy body and mind.

Sleep

I love sleep! Today's high-paced life and overwhelming demands make many of us put sleep low on our list of priorities, but sleep is vital for overall health and wellness. Feeling tired and cranky are not the only side effects of lost sleep; it also contributes to a slew of medical issues, including heart disease, obesity, depression, chronic stress, and cognitive disorders.

Both the number of hours you sleep and the quality of sleep are important. Aim for seven to nine hours every night and practice good sleep habits, which include:

- establishing a regular bedtime

- exercising regularly

- avoiding stimulants like caffeine close to bedtime

- avoiding alcohol before bedtime

- doing something relaxing before bedtime

Following the Mediterranean DASH diet also serves to help you sleep well. Key foods that support sleep quality include seafood, dairy, nuts, beans, and dark leafy greens. These foods contain a variety of nutrients, such as tryptophan, calcium, folate, and magnesium, which work to help elevate serotonin and melatonin levels and promote better quality sleep. And getting your *zzz*s supports a healthy lifestyle!

 A Mediterranean Menu

Planning out your meals for the week is one of the best ways to set yourself up for success. The recipes are designed so that you can choose your favorites among the chapters and mix and match them as you like. Here is an easy sample menu to get you thinking about all the options available to you.

BREAKFAST

(choose one)

Greek Yogurt Parfait with Granola (page 36)

Egg in a "Pepper Hole" with Avocado (page 29)

LUNCH

(choose one)

Tuscan Bean Soup with Kale (page 80)

Wild Rice Salad with Chickpeas and Pickled Radish (page 70)

DINNER

(choose one)

Citrus-Glazed Salmon with Zucchini Noodles (page 106)

Pistachio Quinoa Salad with Pomegranate
Citrus Vinaigrette (page 64)

Roasted Plums with Nut Crumble (page 145)

SNACKS

(choose one or two)

1 cup vegetables with Roasted Red Pepper Hummus (page 50)

Roasted Za'atar Chickpeas (page 59)

Spiced Maple Nuts (page 61)

ABOUT THE RECIPES

I love cooking and creating healthy recipes. Part of the joy of cooking, and how we gain confidence in the kitchen, is to experiment and try new things. These recipes are not set in stone—feel free to play around, switch up ingredients to better meet your preferences, and have fun!

To help get meals together quicker, here are two easy shortcuts I use often:

Cook bigger batches: Batch cooking simply means that you make a larger amount of a recipe, such as doubling the quantity, so that you can enjoy some now and store some for an easy meal later. Freezing works well for dishes like Turmeric Red Lentil Soup (page 79) and Quinoa Lentil "Meatballs" with Quick Tomato Sauce (page 102). You can also cook a large quantity of a whole grain like quinoa to keep in the refrigerator and enjoy it in various forms and meals all week long.

Prep fruits and vegetables in advance: Spending an hour cutting up your fresh fruits and vegetables and storing them in containers in the refrigerator can help set you up for success over the week so salads and sides come together in a snap.

To help give you more ideas and keep your Mediterranean DASH diet lifestyle on track, look for the following tips throughout the recipes.

Substitution Tip: highlights ingredients that may be swapped out for a variety of reasons, including flavor profile and allergies

Cooking Tip: helpful information that can streamline the dish, making it easier to prepare, cook, or clean up, and increase kitchen confidence

Ingredient Tip: nutrition-related ingredient facts or additional information about selecting, storing, or working with an ingredient

Variation Tip: suggestions for swapping, adding, or changing ingredients to try something new with the recipe and keep things interesting

To help you identify recipes that can address a variety of needs, including special dietary requirements, look for the following labels:

Recipe Key

DF Dairy Free	NF Nut Free	30 30-Minutes
FF Family Friendly	1P One Pot	V Vegan
GF Gluten Free		

Dairy Free: recipes that are free of cow's-milk dairy items

Family Friendly: recipes that can feed a family of four and tend to be good for kids

Gluten Free: recipes that are free of gluten. Be sure to check the labels of items like oats and sausage to ensure they are processed in a gluten-free facility.

Nut Free: recipes that are free of nuts

One Pot: recipes that are prepared using only one pot, baking dish, or sheet pan

30 Minute: recipes that require less than 30 minutes to prepare, start to finish

Vegan: recipes that contain only plant-based ingredients

Now, let's get cooking!

Harissa Shakshuka
with Bell Peppers and
Tomatoes, page 28

CHAPTER 2

Breakfast

Sunny-Side Up Baked Eggs with Swiss Chard, Feta, and Basil

SERVES 4 ▪ PREP TIME: 15 MINUTES ▪ COOK TIME: 10 TO 15 MINUTES

1 tablespoon extra-virgin olive oil, divided

½ red onion, diced

½ teaspoon kosher salt

¼ teaspoon nutmeg

⅛ teaspoon freshly ground black pepper

4 cups Swiss chard, chopped

¼ cup crumbled feta cheese

4 large eggs

¼ cup fresh basil, chopped or cut into ribbons

I always smile at the sight of a sunny-side up yolk. This dish produces smiles galore and also happens to be a great way to get some vegetables in at breakfast. Add a slice of whole-wheat toast for extra fiber—and to soak up the gooey yolk. If you don't have individual 5- or 6-ounce ramekins on hand, you can use a 9- or 10-inch oven-safe skillet and do step 3 in the skillet itself.

1 Preheat the oven to 375°F. Place 4 ramekins on a half sheet pan or in a baking dish and grease lightly with olive oil.

2 Heat the remaining olive oil in a large skillet or sauté pan over medium heat. Add the onion, salt, nutmeg, and pepper and sauté until translucent, about 3 minutes. Add the chard and cook, stirring, until wilted, about 2 minutes.

3 Split the mixture among the 4 ramekins. Add 1 tablespoon feta cheese to each ramekin. Crack 1 egg on top of the mixture in each ramekin. Bake for 10 to 12 minutes, or until the egg white is set.

4 Allow to cool for 1 to 2 minutes, then carefully transfer the eggs from the ramekins to a plate with a fork or spatula. Garnish with the basil.

COOKING TIP: *If you leave the eggs in the ramekins after removing them from the oven, they will continue to cook. If you want to serve the eggs in the ramekins, pull them from the oven a little early (after 8 to 10 minutes) so the yolks do not overcook.*

SUBSTITUTION TIP: *I like to keep bags of prewashed baby greens on hand to add to any number of dishes. You can easily substitute baby spinach or baby kale for the Swiss chard. Prewashed greens make it a quick, effortless swap.*

Per Serving Calories: 140; Total fat: 10g; Saturated fat: 3.5g; Cholesterol: 195mg; Sodium: 370mg; Potassium: 250mg; Total Carbohydrates: 4g; Fiber: 4g; Sugars: 2g; Protein: 9g; Magnesium: 40mg; Calcium: 100mg

Harissa Shakshuka with Bell Peppers and Tomatoes

SERVES 4 ▪ PREP TIME: 10 MINUTES ▪ COOK TIME: 20 MINUTES

1½ tablespoons extra-virgin olive oil

2 tablespoons harissa

1 tablespoon tomato paste

½ onion, diced

1 bell pepper, seeded and diced

3 garlic cloves, minced

1 (28-ounce) can no-salt-added diced tomatoes

½ teaspoon kosher salt

4 large eggs

2 to 3 tablespoons fresh basil, chopped or cut into ribbons

Shakshuka, eggs poached in a tomato-based sauce, is perfect for breakfast, lunch, or dinner. This version features bell peppers and harissa, a spicy chili pepper–based paste. With simple ingredients, this dish is a cinch to pull together, but it looks impressive. I love making this when family or friends are visiting. It's a "nothing-in-the-cupboard" go-to dish that is always a crowd-pleaser. Feel free to replace the pepper with eggplant or zucchini, or any other vegetables you have on hand. Serve with crusty whole-wheat bread to mop up the sauce and yolk.

1 Preheat the oven to 375°F.

2 Heat the olive oil in a 12-inch cast-iron pan or oven-proof skillet over medium heat. Add the harissa, tomato paste, onion, and bell pepper; sauté for 3 to 4 minutes. Add the garlic and cook until fragrant, about 30 seconds. Add the diced tomatoes and salt and simmer for about 10 minutes.

3 Make 4 wells in the sauce and gently break 1 egg into each. Transfer to the oven and bake until the whites are cooked and the yolks are set, 10 to 12 minutes.

4 Allow to cool for 3 to 5 minutes, garnish with the basil, and carefully spoon onto plates.

Per Serving Calories: 190; Total fat: 10g; Saturated fat: 2g; Cholesterol: 185mg; Sodium: 255mg; Potassium: 725mg; Total Carbohydrates: 15g; Fiber: 4g; Sugars: 9g; Protein: 9g; Magnesium: 40mg; Calcium: 75mg

Egg in a "Pepper Hole" with Avocado

SERVES 4 ▪ PREP TIME: 15 MINUTES ▪ COOK TIME: 5 MINUTES

4 bell peppers, any color

1 tablespoon extra-virgin olive oil

8 large eggs

¾ teaspoon kosher salt, divided

¼ teaspoon freshly ground black pepper, divided

1 avocado, peeled, pitted, and diced

¼ cup red onion, diced

¼ cup fresh basil, chopped

Juice of ½ lime

There seem to be an unlimited number of names for egg-in-a-hole, including toad-in-a-hole, egg-in-a-cage, and egg-in-a-frame. The names may differ, but the concept remains the same: It's an egg fried in bread. So why not change up the frame? My version uses bell pepper rings instead of bread and pairs it with a diced avocado salad. I promise, it is equally good.

1 Stem and seed the bell peppers. Cut 2 (2-inch-thick) rings from each pepper. Chop the remaining bell pepper into small dice, and set aside.

2 Heat the olive oil in a large skillet over medium heat. Add 4 bell pepper rings, then crack 1 egg in the middle of each ring. Season with ¼ teaspoon of the salt and ⅛ teaspoon of the black pepper. Cook until the egg whites are mostly set but the yolks are still runny, 2 to 3 minutes. Gently flip and cook 1 additional minute for over easy. Move the egg–bell pepper rings to a platter or onto plates, and repeat with the remaining 4 bell pepper rings.

3 In a medium bowl, combine the avocado, onion, basil, lime juice, reserved diced bell pepper, the remaining ¼ teaspoon kosher salt, and the remaining ⅛ teaspoon black pepper. Divide among the 4 plates.

Per Serving (2 egg-pepper rings) Calories: 270; Total fat: 19g; Saturated fat: 4g; Cholesterol: 370mg; Sodium: 360mg; Potassium: 590mg; Total Carbohydrates: 12g; Fiber: 5g; Sugars: 6g; Protein: 15g; Magnesium: 38mg; Calcium: 75mg

Polenta with Sautéed Chard and Fried Eggs

SERVES 4 ▪ PREP TIME: 5 MINUTES ▪ COOK TIME: 20 MINUTES

FOR THE POLENTA

2½ cups water

½ teaspoon kosher salt

¾ cups whole-grain cornmeal

¼ teaspoon freshly ground black pepper

2 tablespoons grated Parmesan cheese

FOR THE CHARD

1 tablespoon extra-virgin olive oil

1 bunch (about 6 ounces) Swiss chard, leaves and stems chopped and separated

2 garlic cloves, sliced

¼ teaspoon kosher salt

⅛ teaspoon freshly ground black pepper

Lemon juice (optional)

FOR THE EGGS

1 tablespoon extra-virgin olive oil

4 large eggs

This rustic Italian dish is also great for lunch or dinner. Keep whole-grain cornmeal on hand in the pantry—it's super versatile and a good way to add a gluten-free grain to any meal. To shorten prep time, you can find prepared polenta in a tube or log form in the refrigerated section of your local grocery store.

TO MAKE THE POLENTA

1 Bring the water and salt to a boil in a medium saucepan over high heat. Slowly add the cornmeal, whisking constantly.

2 Decrease the heat to low, cover, and cook for 10 to 15 minutes, stirring often to avoid lumps. Stir in the pepper and Parmesan, and divide among 4 bowls.

TO MAKE THE CHARD

3 Heat the oil in a large skillet over medium heat. Add the chard stems, garlic, salt, and pepper; sauté for 2 minutes. Add the chard leaves and cook until wilted, about 3 to 5 minutes.

4 Add a spritz of lemon juice (if desired), toss together, and divide evenly on top of the polenta.

TO MAKE THE EGGS

5 Heat the oil in the same large skillet over medium-high heat. Crack each egg into the skillet, taking care not to crowd the skillet and leaving space between the eggs. Cook until the whites are set and golden around the edges, about 2 to 3 minutes.

6 Serve sunny-side up or flip the eggs over carefully and cook 1 minute longer for over easy. Place one egg on top of the polenta and chard in each bowl.

SUBSTITUTION TIP: *Any greens you like or have on hand will work well in this recipe.*

Per Serving Calories: 310; Total fat: 18g; Saturated fat: 5g; Cholesterol: 375mg; Sodium: 500mg; Potassium: 385mg; Total Carbohydrates: 21g; Fiber: 2g; Sugars: 1g; Protein: 17g; Magnesium: 80mg; Calcium: 120mg

Smoked Salmon Egg Scramble with Dill and Chives

SERVES 2 ▪ PREP TIME: 5 MINUTES ▪ COOK TIME: 5 MINUTES

4 large eggs

1 tablespoon milk

1 tablespoon fresh
chives, minced

1 tablespoon fresh
dill, minced

¼ teaspoon kosher salt

⅛ teaspoon freshly ground
black pepper

2 teaspoons extra-virgin
olive oil

2 ounces smoked salmon,
thinly sliced

Bring brunch home with this fun recipe. While this recipe serves two, the servings are easily increased to accommodate overnight guests. Serve over whole-wheat toast with sliced avocado and a side of cut-up fruit and berries for all-day-long energy.

1 In a large bowl, whisk together the eggs, milk, chives, dill, salt, and pepper.

2 Heat the olive oil in a medium skillet or sauté pan over medium heat. Add the egg mixture and cook for about 3 minutes, stirring occasionally.

3 Add the salmon and cook until the eggs are set but moist, about 1 minute.

SUBSTITUTION TIP: *The milk can be replaced with a milk alternative of your choice, such as almond, soy, or oat milk.*

Per Serving Calories: 325; Total fat: 26g; Saturated fat: 6g; Cholesterol: 399mg; Sodium: 455mg; Potassium: 300mg; Total Carbohydrates: 1g; Fiber: 0g; Sugars: 1g; Protein: 23g; Magnesium: 25mg; Calcium: 90mg

Berry Baked Oatmeal

SERVES 8 • PREP TIME: 10 MINUTES • COOK TIME: 45 TO 50 MINUTES

2 cups gluten-free rolled oats

2 cups (10-ounce bag) frozen mixed berries (blueberries and raspberries work best)

2 cups plain, unsweetened almond milk

1 cup plain Greek yogurt

¼ cup maple syrup

2 tablespoons extra-virgin olive oil

2 teaspoons ground cinnamon

1 teaspoon baking powder

1 teaspoon vanilla extract

½ teaspoon kosher salt

¼ teaspoon ground nutmeg

⅛ teaspoon ground cloves

Say goodbye to boring oatmeal! Baked oatmeal's firmer texture makes this a scrumptious morning meal. This family-friendly breakfast can easily be portioned out and frozen; just heat up and serve when needed. For best results, freeze up to 3 months, allow to thaw in the refrigerator, and microwave 2 to 3 minutes to reheat. Try diced apples or pears instead of the frozen berries.

1 Preheat the oven to 375°F.

2 Mix all the ingredients together in a large bowl. Pour into a 9-by-13-inch baking dish. Bake for 45 to 50 minutes, or until golden brown.

Per Serving Calories: 180; Total fat: 6g; Saturated fat: 1g; Cholesterol: 0mg; Sodium: 180mg; Potassium: 50mg; Total Carbohydrates: 28g; Fiber: 4g; Sugars: 11g; Protein: 6g; Magnesium: 4mg; Calcium: 180mg

Fig and Ricotta Toast with Walnuts and Honey

SERVES 2 ▪ PREP TIME: 5 MINUTES

¼ cup ricotta cheese

2 pieces whole-wheat
bread, toasted

4 figs, halved

2 tablespoons
walnuts, chopped

1 teaspoon honey

Fresh figs have a complex texture with their smooth skin, chewy flesh, and crunchy seeds. This fiber- and potassium-rich fruit is available in a few different varieties, ranging in color and size, and are generally in season June through September. Can't find figs? Apricots make a great substitution.

1 Spread 2 tablespoons of ricotta cheese on each piece of toast. Add 4 fig halves to each piece of toast, pressing firmly to keep the figs in the ricotta.

2 Sprinkle 1 tablespoon of walnuts and drizzle ½ teaspoon of honey on each piece of toast.

Per Serving Calories: 215; Total fat: 10g; Saturated fat: 3g; Cholesterol: 16mg; Sodium: 125mg; Potassium: 230mg; Total Carbohydrates: 26g; Fiber: 3g; Sugars: 9g; Protein: 7g; Magnesium: 43mg; Calcium: 92mg

Avocado Toast with Smoked Trout

SERVES 2 ▪ PREP TIME: 10 MINUTES

1 avocado, peeled and pitted

2 teaspoons lemon juice, plus more for serving

¾ teaspoon ground cumin

¼ teaspoon kosher salt

¼ teaspoon red pepper flakes, plus more for sprinkling

¼ teaspoon lemon zest

2 pieces whole-wheat bread, toasted

1 (3.75-ounce) can smoked trout

Take your avocado toast to the next level by adding flavorful spices, citrus, and smoked fish for a healthy boost of omega-3 fatty acids, which are thought to support a healthy brain. So, go ahead and conquer that crossword puzzle after breakfast!

1 In a medium bowl, mash together the avocado, lemon juice, cumin, salt, red pepper flakes, and lemon zest.

2 Spread half the avocado mixture on each piece of toast. Top each piece of toast with half the smoked trout. Garnish with a pinch of red pepper flakes (if desired), and/or a sprinkle of lemon juice (if desired).

SUBSTITUTION TIP: *Any smoked fish makes a nice addition to this avocado toast recipe. There are many varieties available, such as sardines, salmon, or whitefish. Not a fan of smoked fish? A sliced hardboiled egg is a great substitute as well.*

Per Serving Calories: 300; Total fat: 20g; Saturated fat: 3g; Cholesterol: 23mg; Sodium: 390mg; Potassium: 455mg; Total Carbohydrates: 21g; Fiber: 6g; Sugars: 1g; Protein: 11g; Magnesium: 45mg; Calcium: 50mg

Greek Yogurt Parfait with Granola

SERVES: 4 PARFAITS (PLUS EXTRA GRANOLA) ▪ PREP TIME: 10 MINUTES
COOK TIME: 30 MINUTES

FOR THE GRANOLA

¼ cup honey or
    maple syrup

2 tablespoons vegetable oil

2 teaspoons vanilla extract

½ teaspoon kosher salt

3 cups gluten-free
    rolled oats

1 cup mixed raw and
    unsalted nuts, chopped

¼ cup sunflower seeds

1 cup unsweetened
    dried cherries

FOR THE PARFAIT

2 cups plain Greek yogurt

1 cup fresh fruit, chopped
    (optional)

Granola done right is an easy way to add fiber, whole grains, and healthy fats to your morning routine. Making your own granola cuts down on needlessly added salt and sugar and can be customized with any nuts and seeds you like. You can layer the granola with fruit and yogurt for a parfait, eat it like cereal in a bowl with milk, or take it with you on the go for a healthy snack.

TO MAKE THE GRANOLA

1 Preheat the oven to 325°F. Line a baking sheet with parchment paper or foil.

2 Heat the honey, oil, vanilla, and salt in a small saucepan over medium heat. Simmer for 2 minutes and stir together well.

3 In a large bowl, combine the oats, nuts, and seeds. Pour the warm oil mixture over the top and toss well. Spread in a single layer on the prepared baking sheet. Bake for 30 minutes, stirring halfway through. Remove from the oven and add in the dried cherries. Cool completely and store in an airtight container at room temperature for up to 3 months.

TO MAKE THE PARFAIT

For one serving: In a bowl or lowball drinking glass, spoon in ½ cup yogurt, ½ cup granola, and ¼ cup fruit (if desired). Layer in whatever pattern you like.

Per Serving Calories: 370; Total fat: 144g; Saturated fat: 1g; Cholesterol: 6mg; Sodium: 100mg; Potassium: 360mg; Total Carbohydrates: 44g; Fiber: 6g; Sugars: 21g; Protein: 19g; Magnesium: 70mg; Calcium: 175mg

Quinoa Breakfast Bowl with Yogurt, Dates, and Almonds

SERVES 4 ▪ PREP TIME: 10 MINUTES ▪ COOK TIME: 10 TO 12 MINUTES

1½ cups water

1 cup quinoa

2 cinnamon sticks

1-inch knob of
ginger, peeled

¼ teaspoon kosher salt

1 cup plain Greek yogurt

½ cup dates, pitted
and chopped

½ cup almonds (raw or
roasted), chopped

2 teaspoons
honey (optional)

Take a break from oatmeal with this quinoa breakfast bowl. In this recipe, we use yogurt for creaminess, dates for a touch of sweetness, almonds for a bit of crunch, and cinnamon and ginger for a hint of spice. The quinoa flavor and texture are an important part of this dish, so for best results do use quinoa instead of substituting a different grain.

1 Bring the water, quinoa, cinnamon sticks, ginger, and salt to a boil in a medium saucepan over high heat. Reduce the heat to a simmer and cover; simmer for 10 to 12 minutes. Remove the cinnamon sticks and ginger. Fluff with a fork.

2 Add the yogurt, dates, and almonds to the quinoa and mix together. Divide evenly among 4 bowls and garnish with ½ teaspoon honey per bowl, if desired.

SUBSTITUTION TIP: *Use any nuts or seeds you like in place of the almonds.*

Per Serving Calories: 280; Total fat: 11g; Saturated fat: 1g; Cholesterol: 3mg; Sodium: 100mg; Potassium: 450mg; Total Carbohydrates: 37g; Fiber: 6g; Sugars: 18g; Protein: 13g; Magnesium: 110mg; Calcium: 130mg

Berry Warming Smoothie

SERVES 1 ■ PREP TIME: 5 MINUTES

⅔ cup plain kefir or
  plain yogurt

½ cup frozen mixed berries

½ cup baby spinach

½ cup cucumber, chopped

2 tablespoons unsweetened
  shredded coconut

¼ teaspoon grated ginger

¼ teaspoon
  ground cinnamon

¼ teaspoon ground nutmeg

⅛ teaspoon
  ground cardamom

¼ teaspoon vanilla
  extract (optional)

This recipe is packed with a healthy dose of fruits and vegetables, not to mention the probiotics, protein, and calcium from the kefir (fermented cow's milk, similar to a thin yogurt). Smoothies are different from juices in that they use the whole food, which keeps the nutritious skin, pulp, and fiber intact. This also keeps you feeling satisfied longer and provides a slower release of natural sugar into the bloodstream.

In a blender or Vitamix, add all the ingredients. Blend to combine.

Per Serving Calories: 165; Total fat: 7g; Saturated fat: 5g; Cholesterol: 7mg; Sodium: 100mg; Potassium: 115mg; Total Carbohydrates: 20g; Fiber: 4g; Sugars: 16g; Protein: 7g; Magnesium: 10mg; Calcium: 170mg

Almond Butter Banana Chocolate Smoothie

SERVES 1 ▪ PREP TIME: 5 MINUTES

¾ cup almond milk

½ medium banana, preferably frozen

¼ cup frozen blueberries

1 tablespoon almond butter

1 tablespoon unsweetened cocoa powder

1 tablespoon chia seeds

This family-friendly smoothie is reminiscent of a chocolate nut butter cup and is easily batched up for more than a single serving. The cocoa flavor brings the bittersweetness of dark chocolate and adds antioxidants, while the almond butter contributes a nutty creaminess that pairs beautifully with the cocoa and fruit. Chia seeds add a boost of calcium and protein, and help to thicken the smoothie.

In a blender or Vitamix, add all the ingredients. Blend to combine.

SUBSTITUTION TIP: *Allergic to almonds? Swap out the almond milk for any other milk you prefer, such as cow, soy, or oat milk. Peanut butter, sunflower seed butter, and other nut butters are good choices to replace the almond butter.*

Per Serving Calories: 300; Total fat: 16g; Saturated fat: 1g; Cholesterol: 0mg; Sodium: 125mg; Potassium: 450mg; Total Carbohydrates: 37g; Fiber: 10g; Sugars: 17g; Protein: 8g; Magnesium: 100mg; Calcium: 460mg

Roasted Rosemary
Olives, page 60

CHAPTER 3

Snacks, Sides, and Small Plates

Summer Squash Ribbons with Lemon and Ricotta

SERVES 4 ▪ PREP TIME: 20 MINUTES

2 medium zucchini or
   yellow squash

½ cup ricotta cheese

2 tablespoons fresh mint,
   chopped, plus additional
   mint leaves for garnish

2 tablespoons fresh
   parsley, chopped

Zest of ½ lemon

2 teaspoons lemon juice

½ teaspoon kosher salt

¼ teaspoon freshly ground
   black pepper

1 tablespoon extra-virgin
   olive oil

This is a perfect way to use summer's bounty of zucchini, yellow squash, and herbs. It makes a stellar side dish to accompany a piece of roast chicken or fish, or becomes a vegetarian main when mixed with warm whole grains such as farro or whole-wheat spaghetti. For extra texture or crunch, sprinkle toasted chopped walnuts on top.

1 Using a vegetable peeler, make ribbons by peeling the summer squash lengthwise. The squash ribbons will resemble the wide pasta, pappardelle.

2 In a medium bowl, combine the ricotta cheese, mint, parsley, lemon zest, lemon juice, salt, and black pepper.

3 Place mounds of the squash ribbons evenly on 4 plates then dollop the ricotta mixture on top. Drizzle with the olive oil and garnish with the mint leaves.

Per Serving Calories: 90; Total fat: 6g; Saturated fat: 2g; Cholesterol: 10mg; Sodium: 180mg; Potassium: 315mg; Total Carbohydrates: 5g; Fiber: 1g; Sugars: 3g; Protein: 5g; Magnesium: 25mg; Calcium: 105mg

Sautéed Kale with Tomato and Garlic

SERVES 4 ▪ PREP TIME: 5 MINUTES ▪ COOK TIME: 10 MINUTES

1 tablespoon extra-virgin
 olive oil

4 garlic cloves, sliced

¼ teaspoon red
 pepper flakes

2 bunches kale, stemmed
 and chopped or torn
 into pieces

1 (14.5-ounce) can no-salt-
 added diced tomatoes

½ teaspoon kosher salt

Combining different foods not only produces depth of flavor but also something called nutrient synergy—when nutrients from different foods complement each other to create health benefits. This recipe is a great example of this principle. Here, the vitamin C–rich tomatoes serve a very important role; they help optimize the amount of iron we absorb from the kale. Our bodies are less adept at absorbing iron from plant foods (versus animal sources of iron), but we do a lot better with the help of foods rich in vitamin C. This is important because iron is an essential component of hemoglobin, the part of red blood cells that delivers oxygen to all the cells in your body.

1 Heat the olive oil in a wok or large skillet over medium-high heat. Add the garlic and red pepper flakes, and sauté until fragrant, about 30 seconds. Add the kale and sauté, about 3 to 5 minutes, until the kale shrinks down a bit.

2 Add the tomatoes and the salt, stir together, and cook for 3 to 5 minutes, or until the liquid reduces and the kale cooks down further and becomes tender.

INGREDIENT TIP: *Adding garlic and red pepper flakes to the oil first allows the flavors to permeate the oil, creating more flavor for the overall dish. If this makes the dish too spicy for your palate, eliminate the red pepper flakes or add them in step 2 with the salt and tomatoes.*

Per Serving Calories: 110; Total fat: 5g; Saturated fat: 1g; Cholesterol: 0mg; Sodium: 222mg; Potassium: 535mg; Total Carbohydrates: 15g; Fiber: 6g; Sugars: 6g; Protein: 6g; Magnesium: 50mg; Calcium: 182mg

Roasted Broccoli with Tahini Yogurt Sauce

SERVES 4 ▪ PREP TIME: 15 MINUTES ▪ COOK TIME: 30 MINUTES

FOR THE BROCCOLI

1½ to 2 pounds broccoli, stalk trimmed and cut into slices, head cut into florets

1 lemon, sliced into ¼-inch-thick rounds

3 tablespoons extra-virgin olive oil

½ teaspoon kosher salt

¼ teaspoon freshly ground black pepper

FOR THE TAHINI YOGURT SAUCE

½ cup plain Greek yogurt

2 tablespoons tahini

1 tablespoon lemon juice

¼ teaspoon kosher salt

1 teaspoon sesame seeds, for garnish (optional)

Roasted broccoli is a weeknight favorite in my house, on regular rotation at least twice a week. One of my favorite ways to add flavor to broccoli is to pair it with a tahini yogurt sauce. Tahini is a paste made from sesame seeds, which may sound exotic, but it's a staple ingredient in Mediterranean favorites like hummus. Look for it in the condiments or ethnic foods aisle at your local grocery store.

TO MAKE THE BROCCOLI

1 Preheat the oven to 425°F. Line a baking sheet with parchment paper or foil.

2 In a large bowl, gently toss the broccoli, lemon slices, olive oil, salt, and black pepper to combine. Arrange the broccoli in a single layer on the prepared baking sheet. Roast 15 minutes, stir, and roast another 15 minutes, until golden brown.

TO MAKE THE TAHINI YOGURT SAUCE

3 In a medium bowl, combine the yogurt, tahini, lemon juice, and salt; mix well.

4 Spread the tahini yogurt sauce on a platter or large plate and top with the broccoli and lemon slices. Garnish with the sesame seeds (if desired).

COOKING TIP: *Lining your baking sheet with parchment paper or foil makes cleanup a breeze. Simply crumple up and throw away with no need to scrub brown bits off the pan.*

Per Serving Calories: 245; Total fat: 16g; Saturated fat: 2g; Cholesterol: 2mg; Sodium: 305mg; Potassium: 835mg; Total Carbohydrates: 20g; Fiber: 7g; Sugars: 6g; Protein: 12g; Magnesium: 65mg; Calcium: 185mg

Green Beans with Pine Nuts and Garlic

SERVES 4 TO 6 ▪ PREP TIME: 10 MINUTES ▪ COOK TIME: 20 MINUTES

1 pound green
    beans, trimmed

1 head garlic (10 to
    12 cloves), smashed

2 tablespoons extra-virgin
    olive oil

½ teaspoon kosher salt

¼ teaspoon red
    pepper flakes

1 tablespoon white
    wine vinegar

¼ cup pine nuts, toasted

This easy vegetable side is perfect for a party, a quick weeknight dinner, or your holiday table. The roasted green beans come out perfectly charred and tender in this simple recipe. The dish is so good I could eat the whole batch! There's nothing better than a heaping platter of these beauties paired with sweet, mellow whole roasted garlic cloves and crunchy, toasty pine nuts.

1 Preheat the oven to 425°F. Line a baking sheet with parchment paper or foil.

2 In a large bowl, combine the green beans, garlic, olive oil, salt, and red pepper flakes and mix together. Arrange in a single layer on the baking sheet. Roast for 10 minutes, stir, and roast for another 10 minutes, or until golden brown.

3 Mix the cooked green beans with the vinegar and top with the pine nuts.

COOKING TIP: *To cut down on prep time, purchase pretrimmed green beans. They are typically sold in 1-pound bags in the vegetable area at your local grocery store.*

Per Serving Calories: 165; Total fat: 13g; Saturated fat: 1g; Cholesterol: 0mg; Sodium: 150mg; Potassium: 325mg; Total Carbohydrates: 12g; Fiber: 4g; Sugars: 4g; Protein: 4g; Magnesium: 52mg; Calcium: 60mg

Roasted Harissa Carrots

SERVES 4 ▪ PREP TIME: 10 MINUTES ▪ COOK TIME: 15 MINUTES

- 1 pound carrots, peeled and sliced into 1-inch-thick rounds
- 2 tablespoons extra-virgin olive oil
- 2 tablespoons harissa
- 1 teaspoon honey
- 1 teaspoon ground cumin
- ½ teaspoon kosher salt
- ½ cup fresh parsley, chopped

Up your carrot game with this sweet and spicy recipe that takes carrots from lackluster to lovely in minutes. Swap out the honey for maple syrup to make this recipe vegan and add a different dimension to the dish. Pair this with Crispy Mediterranean Chicken Thighs (page 126) and Quinoa with Zucchini, Mint, and Pistachios (page 72) to create a perfectly balanced meal.

1 Preheat the oven to 450°F. Line a baking sheet with parchment paper or foil.

2 In a large bowl, combine the carrots, olive oil, harissa, honey, cumin, and salt. Arrange in a single layer on the baking sheet. Roast for 15 minutes. Remove from the oven, add the parsley, and toss together.

Per Serving Calories: 120; Total fat: 8g; Saturated fat: 1g; Cholesterol: 0mg; Sodium: 255mg; Potassium: 415mg; Total Carbohydrates: 13g; Fiber: 4g; Sugars: 7g; Protein: 1g; Magnesium: 18mg; Calcium: 53mg

Cucumbers with Feta, Mint, and Sumac

SERVES 4 ■ PREP TIME: 15 MINUTES

1 tablespoon extra-virgin
   olive oil

1 tablespoon lemon juice

2 teaspoons ground sumac

½ teaspoon kosher salt

2 hothouse or English
   cucumbers, diced

¼ cup crumbled
   feta cheese

1 tablespoon fresh
   mint, chopped

1 tablespoon fresh
   parsley, chopped

⅛ teaspoon red
   pepper flakes

Crisp and refreshing, the humble cucumber is one of my favorite vegetables. This recipe provides a cooling crunch for your warm weather meals and is an easy side dish for your next cookout or to pack for lunch. If you don't have sumac, substitute lemon or orange zest.

1 In a large bowl, whisk together the olive oil, lemon juice, sumac, and salt. Add the cucumber and feta cheese and toss well.

2 Transfer to a serving dish and sprinkle with the mint, parsley, and red pepper flakes.

Per Serving Calories: 85; Total fat: 6g; Saturated fat: 2g; Cholesterol: 8mg; Sodium: 230mg; Potassium: 295mg; Total Carbohydrates: 8g; Fiber: 1g; Sugars: 4g; Protein: 3g; Magnesium: 27mg; Calcium: 80mg

Cherry Tomato Bruschetta

SERVES 4 ▪ PREP TIME: 15 MINUTES

8 ounces assorted cherry tomatoes, halved

⅓ cup fresh herbs, chopped (such as basil, parsley, tarragon, dill)

1 tablespoon extra-virgin olive oil

¼ teaspoon kosher salt

⅛ teaspoon freshly ground black pepper

¼ cup ricotta cheese

4 slices whole-wheat bread, toasted

Wanna know the best part of bruschetta? Its incredible versatility! Whether you want a snack, an appetizer, or a light meal, it works. This cherry tomato bruschetta is divine, especially during the summer tomato season. All you need are a few ingredients and some fresh bread. If you prefer the dish without bread, simply mix the tomatoes, herbs, olive oil, salt, and black pepper together and serve as a side dish topped with a dollop of ricotta cheese.

1 Combine the tomatoes, herbs, olive oil, salt, and black pepper in a medium bowl and mix gently.

2 Spread 1 tablespoon of ricotta cheese onto each slice of toast. Spoon one-quarter of the tomato mixture onto each bruschetta. If desired, garnish with more herbs.

Per Serving Calories: 100; Total fat: 6g; Saturated fat: 1g; Cholesterol: 5mg; Sodium: 135mg; Potassium: 210mg; Total Carbohydrates: 10g; Fiber: 2g; Sugars: 2g; Protein: 4g; Magnesium: 22mg; Calcium: 60mg

Roasted Red Pepper Hummus

MAKES ABOUT 2 CUPS ■ PREP TIME: 15 MINUTES

1 (15-ounce) can
   low-sodium chickpeas,
   drained and rinsed

3 ounces jarred roasted red
   bell peppers, drained

3 tablespoons tahini

3 tablespoons lemon juice

1 garlic clove, peeled

¾ teaspoon kosher salt

¼ teaspoon freshly ground
   black pepper

3 tablespoons extra-virgin
   olive oil

¼ teaspoon cayenne
   pepper (optional)

Fresh herbs, chopped, for
   garnish (optional)

Rich in healthy fats like olive oil and tahini, hummus is a staple of the Mediterranean diet. Hummus is typically a velvety smooth dip or spread made with five simple ingredients: chickpeas, tahini, lemon, garlic, and olive oil. The addition of roasted red peppers gives this version a flavor twist. For a spicy kick, add in the cayenne pepper. Serve the hummus with warm pita bread and sliced vegetables.

In a food processor, add the chickpeas, red bell peppers, tahini, lemon juice, garlic, salt, and black pepper. Pulse 5 to 7 times. Add the olive oil and process until smooth. Add the cayenne pepper and garnish with chopped herbs, if desired.

Per Serving (¼ cup) Calories: 130; Total fat: 8g; Saturated fat: 1g; Cholesterol: 0mg; Sodium: 150mg; Potassium: 125mg; Total Carbohydrates: 11g; Fiber: 2g; Sugars: 1g; Protein: 4g; Magnesium: 20mg; Calcium: 48mg

Baked Eggplant Baba Ganoush

MAKES ABOUT 4 CUPS ▪ PREP TIME: 10 MINUTES ▪ COOK TIME: 1 HOUR

2 pounds (about 2 medium to large) eggplant

3 tablespoons tahini

Zest of 1 lemon

2 tablespoons lemon juice

¾ teaspoon kosher salt

½ teaspoon ground sumac, plus more for sprinkling (optional)

⅓ cup fresh parsley, chopped

1 tablespoon extra-virgin olive oil

Baba ganoush is a classic Mediterranean dip made with eggplant. I like to bake eggplant whole, until the skin gets wrinkly and the interior flesh steams and becomes silky smooth. Similar to hummus, baba ganoush is best served with sliced vegetables or pita bread. For a crunchy twist, make pita chips by cutting pita bread into wedges, tossing them with olive oil, and broiling them for 1 to 2 minutes per side.

1 Preheat the oven to 350°F. Place the eggplants directly on the rack and bake for 60 minutes, or until the skin is wrinkly.

2 In a food processor add the tahini, lemon zest, lemon juice, salt, and sumac. Carefully cut open the baked eggplant and scoop the flesh into the food processor. Process until the ingredients are well blended.

3 Place in a serving dish and mix in the parsley. Drizzle with the olive oil and sprinkle with sumac, if desired.

Per Serving (½ cup) Calories: 50; Total fat: 4g; Saturated fat: 1g; Cholesterol: 0mg; Sodium: 110mg; Potassium: 42mg; Total Carbohydrates: 2g; Fiber: 1g; Sugars: 0g; Protein: 1g; Magnesium: 7mg; Calcium: 28mg

White Bean Romesco Dip

MAKES ABOUT 4 CUPS ■ PREP TIME: 10 MINUTES

2 red bell peppers, or
  1 (12-ounce) jar roasted
  sweet red peppers in
  water, drained

2 garlic cloves, peeled

½ cup roasted
  unsalted almonds

1 6-inch multigrain pita,
  torn into small pieces

1 teaspoon red
  pepper flakes

1 (14.5-ounce) can no-salt-
  added diced tomatoes

1 (14.5-ounce) can
  low-sodium cannellini
  beans, drained
  and rinsed

1 tablespoon fresh
  parsley, chopped

1 teaspoon sweet or
  smoked paprika

1 teaspoon kosher salt

¼ teaspoon black pepper

¼ cup extra-virgin olive oil

2 tablespoons red
  wine vinegar

2 teaspoons lemon
  juice (optional)

Romesco sauce is typically made from roasted red peppers, tomatoes, almonds, bread, and olive oil. I like to add cannellini beans for a boost of plant-based protein. This makes a great dip for sliced vegetables or to use as a sandwich spread. It also doubles as a pasta sauce—just thin it out to your desired consistency with hot pasta water or vegetable broth. Store the dip in an airtight container in the refrigerator for up to 1 week, or freeze for up to 3 months.

1 If you are using raw peppers, roast them following the steps on page 53 (see Tip), then roughly chop. If using jarred roasted peppers, proceed to step 2.

2 In a food processor, add the garlic and pulse until finely minced. Scrape down the sides of the bowl and add the almonds, pita, and red pepper flakes, and process until minced. Scrape down the sides of the bowl and add the bell peppers, tomatoes, beans, parsley, paprika, salt, and black pepper. Process until smooth.

3 With the food processor running, add the olive oil and vinegar, and process until smooth. Taste, and add the lemon juice to brighten, if desired.

INGREDIENT TIP: *To roast bell peppers, place the whole pepper directly on a gas burner or grill flame, using tongs to turn occasionally. Once the skin is blackened on all sides, carefully wrap each pepper in plastic wrap and set aside to steam and cool. Unwrap the peppers and peel off the blackened skin under cold running water (it should slip right off). Remove the stem, seeds, and membranes, and you're ready to cook.*

Per Serving (½ cup) Calories: 180; Total fat: 10g; Saturated fat: 1g; Cholesterol: 0mg; Sodium: 285mg; Potassium: 270mg; Total Carbohydrates: 20g; Fiber: 4g; Sugars: 3g; Protein: 6g; Magnesium: 40mg; Calcium: 65mg

Roasted Cherry Tomato Caprese

SERVES 4 ▪ PREP TIME: 15 MINUTES ▪ COOK TIME: 30 MINUTES

2 pints (about 20 ounces) cherry tomatoes

6 thyme sprigs

6 garlic cloves, smashed

2 tablespoons extra-virgin olive oil

½ teaspoon kosher salt

8 ounces fresh, unsalted mozzarella, cut into bite-size slices

¼ cup basil, chopped or cut into ribbons

Loaf of crusty whole-wheat bread for serving

One of my favorite summer dishes is a fresh heirloom tomato and mozzarella caprese salad. This version reimagines the traditional caprese salad into a warm dish using cherry tomatoes, whole cloves of garlic, and sprigs of thyme. Roasting helps concentrate the flavor of the tomatoes and mellows out the garlic, creating a sweet, acidic juiciness that pairs perfectly with fresh mozzarella cheese. Serve with crusty whole-wheat bread to soak up the sauce.

1 Preheat the oven to 350°F. Line a baking sheet with parchment paper or foil.

2 Put the tomatoes, thyme, garlic, olive oil, and salt into a large bowl and mix together. Place on the prepared baking sheet in a single layer. Roast for 30 minutes, or until the tomatoes are bursting and juicy.

3 Place the mozzarella on a platter or in a bowl. Pour all the tomato mixture, including the juices, over the mozzarella. Garnish with the basil.

4 Serve with crusty bread.

INGREDIENT TIP: *Multicolored cherry and grape tomatoes help make this dish more colorful without changing the flavor.*

COOKING TIP: *Line the baking sheet with parchment or foil to make transferring the roasted tomatoes and their juices to the final dish easier. Gather up the corners and sides of the parchment, creating a makeshift bowl, and pour the tomatoes over the mozzarella without creating a mess.*

Per Serving (excluding bread) Calories: 250; Total fat: 17g; Saturated fat: 7g; Cholesterol: 31mg; Sodium: 157mg; Potassium: 425mg; Total Carbohydrates: 9g; Fiber: 2g; Sugars: 4g; Protein: 17g; Magnesium: 35mg; Calcium: 445mg

Italian Crepe with Herbs and Onion

SERVES 6 ▪ PREP TIME: 15 MINUTES, PLUS 30 MINUTES TO REST
COOK TIME: 20 MINUTES PER CREPE

2 cups cold water

1 cup chickpea flour

½ teaspoon kosher salt

¼ teaspoon freshly ground
black pepper

3½ tablespoons extra-virgin
olive oil, divided

½ onion, julienned

½ cup fresh herbs, chopped
(thyme, sage, and
rosemary are all nice on
their own or as a mix)

This Italian crepe is known as *farinata*, a thin, crispy-edged, pizza-like pancake made from chickpea flour. I first came across this in Italy and then again at a Mediterranean restaurant in Arizona. It was by far the best thing we ate on that trip, and I became obsessed with trying to make it at home. This recipe uses what I discovered to be the best method. Many grocery stores carry chickpea flour in the ethnic or gluten-free areas of the store, but if you cannot find it there, it is also readily available online.

1 In a large bowl, whisk together the water, flour, salt, and black pepper. Add 2 tablespoons of the olive oil and whisk. Let the batter sit at room temperature for at least 30 minutes.

2 Preheat the oven to 450°F. Place a 12-inch cast-iron pan or oven-safe skillet in the oven to warm as the oven comes to temperature.

3 Remove the hot pan from the oven carefully, add ½ tablespoon of the olive oil and one-third of the onion, stir, and place the pan back in the oven. Cook, stirring occasionally, until the onions are golden brown, 5 to 8 minutes.

4 Remove the pan from the oven and pour in one-third of the batter (about 1 cup), sprinkle with one-third of the herbs, and put it back in the oven. Bake for 10 minutes, or until firm and the edges are set.

5 Increase the oven setting to broil and cook 3 to 5 minutes, or until golden brown. Slide the crepe onto the cutting board and repeat twice more. Halve the crepes and cut into wedges. Serve warm or at room temperature.

COOKING TIP: *Batter can be made ahead of time and kept in the refrigerator up to 5 days. When ready to use, remove from the refrigerator, whisk well, and let sit for 15 minutes.*

VARIATION TIP: *This basic crepe recipe works well with a variety of toppings and mix-ins. Try red onions and sliced olives, or basil with chopped tomatoes and feta as a topping after it has finished cooking.*

Per Serving Calories: 135; Total fat: 9g; Saturated fat: 1g; Cholesterol: 0mg; Sodium: 105mg; Potassium: 165mg; Total Carbohydrates: 11g; Fiber: 2g; Sugars: 2g; Protein: 4g; Magnesium: 30mg; Calcium: 20mg

Pita Pizza with Olives, Feta, and Red Onion

SERVES 4 ▪ PREP TIME: 15 MINUTES ▪ COOK TIME: 10 MINUTES

4 (6-inch) whole-wheat pitas

1 tablespoon extra-virgin olive oil

½ cup hummus (store-bought or Roasted Red Pepper Hummus, page 50)

½ bell pepper, julienned

½ red onion, julienned

¼ cup olives, pitted and chopped

¼ cup crumbled feta cheese

¼ teaspoon red pepper flakes

¼ cup fresh herbs, chopped (mint, parsley, oregano, or a mix)

Pita pizzas are sure to be a hit with all ages and can be served as a snack, appetizer, or as part of the main meal. Feel free to experiment with your toppings; try chopped tomatoes and sliced mushrooms instead of the pepper and onion. Just be careful not to overload each pita with toppings, which will cause them to steam and be soggy rather than charred. Whole-wheat pitas without pockets work well for this recipe.

1 Preheat the broiler to low. Line a baking sheet with parchment paper or foil.

2 Place the pitas on the prepared baking sheet and brush both sides with the olive oil. Broil 1 to 2 minutes per side until starting to turn golden brown.

3 Spread 2 tablespoons hummus on each pita. Top the pitas with bell pepper, onion, olives, feta cheese, and red pepper flakes. Broil again until the cheese softens and starts to get golden brown, 4 to 6 minutes, being careful not to burn the pitas.

4 Remove from broiler and top with the herbs.

Per Serving Calories: 185; Total fat: 11g; Saturated fat: 2g; Cholesterol: 8mg; Sodium: 285mg; Potassium: 13mg; Total Carbohydrates: 17g; Fiber: 3g; Sugars: 3g; Protein: 5g; Magnesium: 18mg; Calcium: 91mg

Roasted Za'atar Chickpeas

SERVES 8 ■ PREP TIME: 5 MINUTES ■ COOK TIME: 1 HOUR

3 tablespoons za'atar

2 tablespoons extra-virgin olive oil

½ teaspoon kosher salt

¼ teaspoon freshly ground black pepper

4 cups cooked chickpeas, or 2 (15-ounce) cans, drained and rinsed

These crunchy, fiber-rich chickpeas are perfect for a snack, party appetizer, or as topping on a salad. This simple recipe uses za'atar as the main spice, but you can try other spices or whatever you have on hand. For a spicier mix, try a little cayenne pepper. Dried sage adds a touch of herby sweetness. For smokiness, add a dash of smoked paprika.

1 Preheat the oven to 400°F. Line a baking sheet with foil or parchment paper.

2 In a large bowl, combine the za'atar, olive oil, salt, and black pepper. Add the chickpeas and mix thoroughly.

3 Spread the chickpeas in a single layer on the prepared baking sheet. Bake for 45 to 60 minutes, or until golden brown and crispy. Cool and store in an airtight container at room temperature for up to 1 week.

Per Serving Calories: 150; Total fat: 6g; Saturated fat: 1g; Cholesterol: 0mg; Sodium: 230mg; Potassium: 182mg; Total Carbohydrates: 17g; Fiber 6g; Sugars: 3g; Protein: 6g; Magnesium: 32mg; Calcium: 52mg

Roasted Rosemary Olives

SERVES 4 ▪ PREP TIME: 5 MINUTES ▪ COOK TIME: 25 MINUTES

1 cup mixed variety olives, pitted and rinsed

2 tablespoons lemon juice

1 tablespoon extra-virgin olive oil

6 garlic cloves, peeled

4 rosemary sprigs

I first tried roasted olives at a New York City tapas restaurant years ago and have been recreating them at home ever since. Roasting vegetables is something I already do several times a week, but olives had never been part of the rotation. I'm always fascinated when I roast olives; some are sweeter, others get mellower, some crunchier, and others slightly chewy. For this reason, I recommend using a variety of olives so that you get a range of flavors and textures. Keep an eye on the garlic and pull the pan out early if it starts to burn.

1 Preheat the oven to 400°F. Line the baking sheet with parchment paper or foil.

2 Combine the olives, lemon juice, olive oil, and garlic in a medium bowl and mix together. Spread in a single layer on the prepared baking sheet. Sprinkle on the rosemary. Roast for 25 minutes, tossing halfway through.

3 Remove the rosemary leaves from the stem and place in a serving bowl. Add the olives and mix before serving.

Per Serving Calories: 100; Total fat: 9g; Saturated fat: 1g; Cholesterol: 0mg; Sodium: 260mg; Potassium: 31mg; Total Carbohydrates: 4g; Fiber: 0g; Sugars: 0g; Protein: 0g; Magnesium: 3mg; Calcium: 11mg

Spiced Maple Nuts

MAKES ABOUT 2 CUPS ▪ PREP TIME: 5 MINUTES ▪ COOK TIME: 10 MINUTES

2 cups raw walnuts or
    pecans (or a mix of nuts)

1 teaspoon extra-virgin
    olive oil

1 teaspoon ground sumac

½ teaspoon pure
    maple syrup

¼ teaspoon kosher salt

¼ teaspoon ground ginger

2 to 4 rosemary sprigs

These Spiced Maple Nuts offer a hint of maple sweetness, warmth from the ginger, and a touch of citrus from the sumac. I prefer walnuts and pecans because their crevices allow more of the spice mixture to bake in, making a more flavorful and toasted combination, but any nuts will work.

1 Preheat the oven to 350°F. Line a baking sheet with parchment paper or foil.

2 In a large bowl, combine the nuts, olive oil, sumac, maple syrup, salt, and ginger; mix together. Spread in a single layer on the prepared baking sheet. Add the rosemary. Roast for 8 to 10 minutes, or until golden and fragrant.

3 Remove the rosemary leaves from the stems and place in a serving bowl. Add the nuts and toss to combine before serving.

Per Serving (¼ cup) Calories: 175; Total fat: 18g; Saturated fat: 2g; Cholesterol: 0mg; Sodium: 35mg; Potassium: 110mg; Total Carbohydrates: 4g; Fiber: 2g; Sugars: 1g; Protein: 3g; Magnesium: 35mg; Calcium: 23mg

Tuscan Bean Soup
with Kale, page 80

CHAPTER 4
Salads and Soups

Pistachio Quinoa Salad with Pomegranate Citrus Vinaigrette

SERVES 6 ▪ PREP TIME: 15 MINUTES ▪ COOK TIME: 15 MINUTES

FOR THE QUINOA
1½ cups water
1 cup quinoa
¼ teaspoon kosher salt

FOR THE DRESSING
1 cup extra-virgin olive oil
½ cup pomegranate juice
½ cup freshly squeezed
    orange juice
1 small shallot, minced
1 teaspoon pure maple syrup
1 teaspoon za'atar
½ teaspoon ground sumac
½ teaspoon kosher salt
¼ teaspoon freshly ground
    black pepper

FOR THE SALAD
3 cups baby spinach
½ cup fresh parsley,
    coarsely chopped
½ cup fresh mint,
    coarsely chopped
Approximately ¾ cup
    pomegranate seeds, or
    2 pomegranates
¼ cup pistachios, shelled
    and toasted
¼ cup crumbled
    blue cheese

This herbaceous grain salad is full of fresh ingredients and delivers a ton of flavor and texture due to the chewy quinoa, the crunchy pistachios, the sweet and sour pop of the pomegranate seeds, and the creamy blue cheese. The dressing blends citrus and pomegranate juices, bringing more cohesiveness to the dish. I always find it useful to make extra dressing, so be sure to save clean glass jars, which are a great way to store dressings. This recipe makes more dressing than you need; store it in the refrigerator for up to 2 weeks.

TO MAKE THE QUINOA

Bring the water, quinoa, and salt to a boil in a small saucepan. Reduce the heat and cover; simmer for 10 to 12 minutes. Fluff with a fork.

TO MAKE THE DRESSING

1 In a medium bowl, whisk together the olive oil, pomegranate juice, orange juice, shallot, maple syrup, za'atar, sumac, salt, and black pepper.

2 In a large bowl, add about ½ cup of dressing.

3 Store the remaining dressing in a glass jar or airtight container and refrigerate. The dressing can be kept up to 2 weeks. Let the chilled dressing reach room temperature before using.

TO MAKE THE SALAD

4 Combine the spinach, parsley, and mint in the bowl with the dressing and toss gently together.

5 Add the quinoa. Toss gently.

6 Add the pomegranate seeds.

7 Or, if using whole pomegranates: Cut the pomegranates in half. Fill a large bowl with water and hold the pomegranate half, cut side-down. Using a wooden spoon, hit the back of the pomegranate so the seeds fall into the water. Immerse the pomegranate in the water and gently pull out any remaining seeds. Repeat with the remaining pomegranate. Skim the white pith off the top of the water. Drain the seeds and add them to the greens.

8 Add the pistachios and cheese and toss gently.

SUBSTITUTION TIP: *You can use any citrus juice you like for the dressing. Try lemon, lime, or grapefruit in place of orange.*

SUBSTITUTION TIP: *Look for sumac and za'atar in the spice aisle of your local grocery. If you cannot find them, make your own mix with equal amounts of sesame seeds, dried thyme, and orange zest.*

Per Serving Calories: 300; Total fat: 19g; Saturated fat: 4g; Cholesterol: 6mg; Sodium: 225mg; Potassium: 520mg; Total Carbohydrates: 28g; Fiber: 5g; Sugars: 8g; Protein: 8g; Magnesium: 85mg; Calcium: 110mg

Cauliflower Tabbouleh Salad

SERVES 4 ▪ PREP TIME: 15 MINUTES

¼ cup extra-virgin olive oil

¼ cup lemon juice

Zest of 1 lemon

¾ teaspoon kosher salt

½ teaspoon
ground turmeric

¼ teaspoon
ground coriander

¼ teaspoon ground cumin

¼ teaspoon black pepper

⅛ teaspoon
ground cinnamon

1 pound riced cauliflower

1 English cucumber, diced

12 cherry tomatoes, halved

1 cup fresh parsley, chopped

½ cup fresh mint, chopped

Traditional tabbouleh is made with bulgur wheat. This variation uses riced cauliflower instead, which is a great way to add more vegetables, vitamins, and minerals. The turmeric, cumin, mint, and parsley contribute a ton of flavor and brightness. Look for riced cauliflower in the produce or frozen aisles at your local grocery store. You can also make your own by grating a head of cauliflower or cutting it into chunks and using your food processor.

1 In a large bowl, whisk together the olive oil, lemon juice, lemon zest, salt, turmeric, coriander, cumin, black pepper, and cinnamon.

2 Add the riced cauliflower to the bowl and mix well. Add in the cucumber, tomatoes, parsley, and mint and gently mix together.

Per Serving Calories: 180; Total fat: 15g; Saturated fat: 2g; Cholesterol: 0mg; Sodium: 260mg; Potassium: 690mg; Total Carbohydrates: 12g; Fiber: 5g; Sugars: 5g; Protein: 4g; Magnesium: 45mg; Calcium: 75mg

Tuna Niçoise

SERVES 4 ▪ PREP TIME: 15 MINUTES ▪ COOK TIME: 20 MINUTES

1 pound small red
   or fingerling
   potatoes, halved

1 pound green beans or
   haricots verts, trimmed

1 head romaine lettuce,
   chopped or torn into
   bite-size pieces

½ pint cherry
   tomatoes, halved

8 radishes, sliced thin

½ cup olives, pitted (any
   kind you like)

2 (5-ounce) cans no-salt-
   added tuna packed in
   olive oil, drained

8 anchovies (optional)

This version of the French bistro staple amps up the vegetables and makes protein-rich tuna the star. It is a composed salad, which means that the ingredients are grouped on a plate rather than tossed together in a bowl, and the dressing is served on the side or drizzled on top. Serve with the Lemon Vinaigrette (page 155), Olive Mint Vinaigrette (page 156), or a simple drizzle of olive oil.

1 Fill a large pot fitted with a steamer basket with 2 to 3 inches of water. Put the potatoes in the steamer basket and lay the green beans on top of the potatoes. Bring the water to a boil over high heat, lower the heat to low and simmer, cover, and cook for 7 minutes, or until the green beans are tender but crisp. Remove the green beans and continue to steam the potatoes for an additional 10 minutes.

2 Place the romaine lettuce on a serving platter. Group the potatoes, green beans, tomatoes, radishes, olives, and tuna in different areas of the platter. If using the anchovies, place them around the platter.

VARIATION TIP: *During the colder months, I like making this dish with roasted potatoes and green beans. Toss the vegetables with olive oil, spread on a baking sheet, and roast for 20 to 30 minutes, at 425°F, turning halfway through.*

Per Serving Calories: 315; Total fat: 9g; Saturated fat: 1g; Cholesterol: 18mg; Sodium: 420mg; Potassium: 1400mg; Total Carbohydrates: 33g; Fiber: 9g; Sugars: 8g; Protein: 28g; Magnesium: 100mg; Calcium: 120mg

Roasted Golden Beet, Avocado, and Watercress Salad

SERVES 4 ▪ PREP TIME: 15 MINUTES ▪ COOK TIME: 1 HOUR

1 bunch (about 1½ pounds) golden beets

1 tablespoon extra-virgin olive oil

1 tablespoon white wine vinegar

½ teaspoon kosher salt

¼ teaspoon freshly ground black pepper

1 bunch (about 4 ounces) watercress

1 avocado, peeled, pitted, and diced

¼ cup crumbled feta cheese

¼ cup walnuts, toasted

1 tablespoon fresh chives, chopped

To avoid staining my fingers dark red, I often choose to prepare golden beets instead of traditional red beets. I can prevent some extra cleanup, while creating a slightly sweeter and less earthy flavor, which may help make fans of the less-than-enthusiastic beet eaters out there. If you cannot find golden beets, Candy-Stripe (or Chioggia) beets are a colorful alternative or, of course, red beets will work just as well.

1 Preheat the oven to 425°F. Wash and trim the beets (cut an inch above the beet root, leaving the long tail if desired), then wrap each beet individually in foil. Place the beets on a baking sheet and roast until fully cooked, 45 to 60 minutes depending on the size of each beet. Start checking at 45 minutes; if easily pierced with a fork, the beets are cooked.

2 Remove the beets from the oven and allow them to cool. Under cold running water, slough off the skin. Cut the beets into bite-size cubes or wedges.

3 In a large bowl, whisk together the olive oil, vinegar, salt, and black pepper. Add the watercress and beets and toss well. Add the avocado, feta, walnuts, and chives and mix gently.

VARIATION TIP: *Looking to make this salad a heartier lunch or dinner? Canned tuna, salmon, or sardines make a great addition.*

SUBSTITUTION TIP: *If you don't have feta, or simply don't like it, goat cheese works just as well here.*

Per Serving Calories: 235; Total fat: 16g; Saturated fat: 3g; Cholesterol: 8mg; Sodium: 365mg; Potassium: 790mg; Total Carbohydrates: 21g; Fiber: 8g; Sugars: 12g; Protein: 6g; Magnesium: 65mg; Calcium: 95mg

Wild Rice Salad with Chickpeas and Pickled Radish

SERVES 4 AS A MAIN OR 6 AS A SIDE ▪ PREP TIME: 20 MINUTES ▪ COOK TIME: 45 MINUTES

FOR THE RICE
1 cup water
4 ounces (⅔ cup) wild rice
¼ teaspoon kosher salt

FOR THE PICKLED RADISH
1 bunch radishes (6 to
    8 small), sliced thin
½ cup white wine vinegar
½ teaspoon kosher salt

FOR THE DRESSING
2 tablespoons extra-virgin
    olive oil
2 tablespoons white
    wine vinegar
½ teaspoon pure
    maple syrup
½ teaspoon kosher salt
¼ teaspoon freshly ground
    black pepper

Most vegetables (and some fruits!) can be quick pickled for added crunch, acidity, and brightness. Quick pickling is a creative way to use up extra produce in your refrigerator. Many components of this dish can be made ahead. The pickled radishes can be refrigerated in an airtight container for up to 2 weeks, and the wild rice can be cooked and mixed with the dressing the day before.

TO MAKE THE RICE

Bring the water, rice, and salt to a boil in a medium saucepan. Cover, reduce the heat, and simmer for 45 minutes.

TO MAKE THE PICKLED RADISH

In a medium bowl, combine the radishes, vinegar, and salt. Let sit for 15 to 30 minutes.

TO MAKE THE DRESSING

In a large bowl, whisk together the olive oil, vinegar, maple syrup, salt, and black pepper.

FOR THE SALAD

1 (15-ounce) can no-salt-added or low-sodium chickpeas, rinsed and drained

1 bulb fennel, diced

¼ cup walnuts, chopped and toasted

¼ cup crumbled feta cheese

¼ cup currants

2 tablespoons fresh dill, chopped

TO MAKE THE SALAD

1 While still warm, add the rice to the bowl with the dressing and mix well.

2 Add the chickpeas, fennel, walnuts, feta, currants, and dill. Mix well.

3 Garnish with the pickled radishes before serving.

SUBSTITUTION TIP: *Try raisins in place of the currants.*

Per Serving Calories: 310; Total fat: 16g; Saturated fat: 3g; Cholesterol: 8mg; Sodium: 400mg; Potassium: 415mg; Total Carbohydrates: 36g; Fiber: 7g; Sugars: 11g; Protein: 10g; Magnesium: 70mg; Calcium: 110mg

Quinoa with Zucchini, Mint, and Pistachios

SERVES 4 ▪ PREP TIME: 20 TO 30 MINUTES ▪ COOK TIME: 20 MINUTES

FOR THE QUINOA

1½ cups water

1 cup quinoa

¼ teaspoon kosher salt

FOR THE SALAD

2 tablespoons extra-virgin olive oil

1 zucchini, thinly sliced into rounds

6 small radishes, sliced

1 shallot, julienned

¾ teaspoon kosher salt

¼ teaspoon freshly ground black pepper

2 garlic cloves, sliced

Zest of 1 lemon

2 tablespoons lemon juice

¼ cup fresh mint, chopped

¼ cup fresh basil, chopped

¼ cup pistachios, shelled and toasted

Cooking radishes tames their bite and brings out their natural earthy flavor. Zucchini and shallots up the vegetable goodness in this recipe while the quinoa lends texture and protein. The lemon juice creates acidity and brightness, and the pistachios add healthy fats and a nutty crunch. A perfect blend of nutrients, flavors, and textures, this simple vegan recipe makes a great meal or side dish. Feel free to swap out the pistachios for other nuts you like and have on hand. Toasted walnuts, pecans, or almonds would be a great addition!

TO MAKE THE QUINOA

Bring the water, quinoa, and salt to a boil in a medium saucepan. Reduce to a simmer, cover, and cook for 10 to 12 minutes. Fluff with a fork.

TO MAKE THE SALAD

1 Heat the olive oil in a large skillet or sauté pan over medium-high heat. Add the zucchini, radishes, shallot, salt, and black pepper, and sauté for 7 to 8 minutes. Add the garlic and cook 30 seconds to 1 minute more.

2 In a large bowl, combine the lemon zest and lemon juice. Add the quinoa and mix well. Add the cooked zucchini mixture and mix well. Add the mint, basil, and pistachios and gently mix.

Per Serving Calories: 220; Total fat: 12g; Saturated fat: 2g; Cholesterol: 0mg; Sodium: 295mg; Potassium: 515mg; Total Carbohydrates: 25g; Fiber: 5g; Sugars: 5g; Protein: 6g; Magnesium: 75mg; Calcium: 55mg

Italian White Bean Salad with Bell Peppers

SERVES 4 ▪ PREP TIME: 15 MINUTES

2 tablespoons extra-virgin olive oil

2 tablespoons white wine vinegar

½ shallot, minced

½ teaspoon kosher salt

¼ teaspoon freshly ground black pepper

3 cups cooked cannellini beans, or 2 (15-ounce) cans no-salt-added or low-sodium cannellini beans, drained and rinsed

2 celery stalks, diced

½ red bell pepper, diced

¼ cup fresh parsley, chopped

¼ cup fresh mint, chopped

Texture and taste are vital components of any meal, and this dish delivers both with cannellini beans, bell pepper, and celery. The beans are a good source of protein, magnesium, and potassium, as well as fiber and phytochemicals, which help heart health. The parsley, mint, and a light dressing round it out. This dish holds up well over time, so make it a day ahead and save any leftovers for lunch.

1 In a large bowl, whisk together the olive oil, vinegar, shallot, salt, and black pepper.

2 Add the beans, celery, red bell pepper, parsley, and mint; mix well.

VARIATION TIP: *To make this salad a heartier lunch or dinner, mix in a cooked whole grain such as farro or sorghum. Adding a dollop of Salsa Verde (page 152) will add new flavors and depth to the dish as well.*

Per Serving Calories: 300; Total fat: 8g; Saturated fat: 1g; Cholesterol: 0mg; Sodium: 175mg; Potassium: 1100mg; Total Carbohydrates: 46g; Fiber: 11g; Sugars: 3g; Protein: 15g; Magnesium: 115mg; Calcium: 175mg

French Lentil Salad with Parsley and Mint

SERVES 4 AS A MAIN OR 6 AS A SIDE ▪ PREP TIME: 20 MINUTES ▪ COOK TIME: 25 MINUTES

FOR THE LENTILS

1 cup French lentils

1 garlic clove, smashed

1 dried bay leaf

FOR THE SALAD

2 tablespoons extra-virgin
olive oil

2 tablespoons red
wine vinegar

½ teaspoon ground cumin

½ teaspoon kosher salt

¼ teaspoon freshly ground
black pepper

2 celery stalks, diced small

1 bell pepper, diced small

½ red onion, diced small

¼ cup fresh
parsley, chopped

¼ cup fresh mint, chopped

French lentils are slightly different from the typical brown or green lentils. For this dish, it is worth paying a little extra for the French lentils. What's the difference? French lentils are slightly darker and smaller than standard lentils. They hold their shape extremely well when cooked, have an al dente bite, and have a slightly richer and more peppery flavor than other lentils. Puy lentils, grown in the Puy region of France, and black beluga lentils will also work well.

TO MAKE THE LENTILS

1 Put the lentils, garlic, and bay leaf in a large saucepan. Cover with water by about 3 inches and bring to a boil. Reduce the heat, cover, and simmer until tender, 20 to 30 minutes.

2 Drain the lentils to remove any remaining water after cooking. Remove the garlic and bay leaf.

TO MAKE THE SALAD

3 In a large bowl, whisk together the olive oil, vinegar, cumin, salt, and black pepper. Add the celery, bell pepper, onion, parsley, and mint and toss to combine.

4 Add the lentils and mix well.

Per Serving Calories: 200; Total fat: 8g; Saturated fat: 1g; Cholesterol: 0mg; Sodium: 165mg; Potassium: 565mg; Total Carbohydrates: 26g; Fiber: 10g; Sugars: 5g; Protein: 10g; Magnesium: 50mg; Calcium: 50mg

Roasted Cauliflower and Arugula Salad with Pomegranate and Pine Nuts

SERVES 4 ▪ PREP TIME: 20 MINUTES ▪ COOK TIME: 20 MINUTES

1 head cauliflower, trimmed and cut into 1-inch florets

2 tablespoons extra-virgin olive oil, plus more for drizzling (optional)

1 teaspoon ground cumin

½ teaspoon kosher salt

¼ teaspoon freshly ground black pepper

5 ounces arugula

⅓ cup pomegranate seeds

¼ cup pine nuts, toasted

Roasted cauliflower provides a golden-brown crunch to this dish, with a caramelized sweet and nutty flavor. Cumin adds heat and helps balance the sweetness of the pomegranate seeds, the spiciness of the arugula, and the richness of the pine nuts. To make this a full meal, add in grilled chicken, sautéed tofu, or canned tuna.

1 Preheat the oven to 425°F. Line a baking sheet with parchment paper or foil.

2 In a large bowl, combine the cauliflower, olive oil, cumin, salt, and black pepper. Spread in a single layer on the prepared baking sheet and roast for 20 minutes, tossing halfway through.

3 Divide the arugula among 4 plates. Top with the cauliflower, pomegranate seeds, and pine nuts.

4 Serve with Lemon Vinaigrette dressing (page 155) or a simple drizzle of olive oil.

Per Serving (excluding dressing) Calories: 190; Total fat: 14g; Saturated fat: 2g; Cholesterol: 0mg; Sodium: 210mg; Potassium: 850mg; Total Carbohydrates: 16g; Fiber: 6g; Sugars: 7g; Protein: 6g; Magnesium: 75mg; Calcium: 110mg

Red Gazpacho

SERVES 4 ▪ PREP TIME: 15 MINUTES

2 pounds tomatoes, cut into chunks

1 bell pepper, cut into chunks

1 cucumber, cut into chunks

1 small red onion, cut into chunks

1 garlic clove, smashed

2 teaspoons sherry vinegar

½ teaspoon kosher salt

¼ teaspoon freshly ground black pepper

⅓ cup extra-virgin olive oil

Lemon juice (optional)

¼ cup fresh chives, chopped, for garnish

Gazpacho is a popular tomato-based cold soup that originated in Spain but is now widely adapted and has come to mean a cold soup with a vegetable or fruit base. This refreshing recipe is jam-packed with vegetables and best made with fresh ingredients. Think of it as a liquid salad, bursting with flavor. Serve it alongside some crusty whole-wheat bread or pita. For an extra dose of protein, garnish with sautéed shrimp.

In a high-speed blender or Vitamix, add the tomatoes, bell pepper, cucumber, onion, garlic, vinegar, salt, and black pepper. Blend until smooth. With the motor running, add the olive oil and purée until smooth. Add more vinegar or a spritz of lemon juice if needed. Garnish with the chives.

SUBSTITUTION TIP: *Any herbs will go nicely with this refreshing cold soup. Use parsley, basil, or whatever you like in place of the chives.*

Per Serving Calories: 240; Total fat: 19g; Saturated fat: 3g; Cholesterol: 0mg; Sodium: 155mg; Potassium: 830mg; Total Carbohydrates: 18g; Fiber: 5g; Sugars: 11g; Protein: 4g; Magnesium: 50mg; Calcium: 60mg

Roasted Eggplant Soup

SERVES 6 ▪ PREP TIME: 15 MINUTES ▪ COOK TIME: 40 MINUTES

Olive oil cooking spray

2 pounds (1 to 2 medium to large) eggplant, halved lengthwise

2 beefsteak tomatoes, halved

2 onions, halved

4 garlic cloves, smashed

4 rosemary sprigs

2 tablespoons extra-virgin olive oil

1 to 2 cups no-salt-added vegetable stock

1 teaspoon pure maple syrup

1 teaspoon ground cumin

1 teaspoon ground coriander

1 teaspoon kosher salt

¼ teaspoon freshly ground black pepper

Lemon juice (optional)

Roasted eggplant, tomatoes, onions, and garlic make this an irresistible vegan soup with more than two standard servings of vegetables in each portion. Roasting the vegetables creates a silky smooth texture and a slightly sweet flavor. The spices add warmth, and the maple syrup rounds it out beautifully. If you prefer a thinner soup, increase the amount of vegetable stock until you reach your desired consistency. You could garnish with crumbled feta or goat cheese to add a bit of salty creaminess.

1 Preheat the oven to 400°F. Line two baking sheets with parchment paper or foil. Lightly spray with olive oil cooking spray. Spread the eggplant, tomatoes, onions, and garlic on the prepared baking sheets, cut-side down. Nestle the rosemary sprigs among the vegetables. Drizzle with the olive oil and roast for 40 minutes, checking halfway through and removing the garlic before it gets brown.

2 When cool enough to touch, remove the eggplant flesh and tomato flesh from the skin and add to a high-powered blender, food processor, or Vitamix. Add the rosemary leaves, onions, garlic, 1 cup of the vegetable stock, maple syrup, cumin, coriander, salt, and black pepper. Purée until smooth. The soup should be thick and creamy. If the soup is too thick, add another cup of stock slowly, until your desired consistency is reached. Spritz with lemon juice, if desired.

Per Serving Calories: 185; Total fat: 8g; Saturated fat: 1g; Cholesterol: 0mg; Sodium: 400mg; Potassium: 1000mg; Total Carbohydrates: 29g; Fiber: 9g; Sugars: 17g; Protein: 4g; Magnesium: 55mg; Calcium: 60mg

Lentil Sweet Potato Soup

SERVES 6 ▪ PREP TIME: 15 MINUTES ▪ COOK TIME: 30 MINUTES

- 1 tablespoon extra-virgin olive oil
- 1 onion, diced
- 1 carrot, diced
- 1 celery stalk, diced
- 1 sweet potato, unpeeled and diced
- 1 cup green or brown lentils
- 1 dried bay leaf
- 1 teaspoon ground turmeric
- 1 teaspoon ground cumin
- 1 teaspoon kosher salt
- ¼ teaspoon freshly ground black pepper
- 4 cups no-salt-added vegetable stock

Earthy lentils, wholesome sweet potatoes, lots of vegetables, and spices add up to a hearty and nourishing soup, perfect for chilly weather. Sweet potatoes are extremely nutritious, chock-full of vitamin B_6 and potassium, which help keep blood pressure in check. I like to leave the peel intact, providing additional fiber to help your digestive tract stay healthy.

1 Heat the olive oil in a large stockpot over medium-high heat. Add the onion, carrot, celery, and sweet potato and sauté 5 to 6 minutes. Add the lentils, bay leaf, turmeric, cumin, salt, and black pepper and cook for 30 seconds to 1 minute more.

2 Add the stock, bring to a boil, then lower the heat to low, and simmer, covered for 20 to 30 minutes, or until the lentils and sweet potato are tender. If you find the soup becoming thick and stew-like, feel free to add additional stock or water as it cooks.

VARIATION TIP: *Herbs are a welcome addition to most dishes. If you have any fresh herbs, feel free to mix in ¼ cup chopped to the finished soup.*

Per Serving Calories: 145; Total fat: 3g; Saturated fat: 0g; Cholesterol: 0mg; Sodium: 350mg; Potassium: 455mg; Total Carbohydrates: 25g; Fiber: 7g; Sugars: 6g; Protein: 7g; Magnesium: 35mg; Calcium: 30mg

Turmeric Red Lentil Soup

SERVES 6 ▪ PREP TIME: 15 MINUTES ▪ COOK TIME: 30 MINUTES

1 tablespoon extra-virgin
olive oil

1 teaspoon ground cumin

1 teaspoon
ground coriander

1 teaspoon ground turmeric

1 teaspoon kosher salt

¼ teaspoon freshly ground
black pepper

1 tablespoon no-salt-added
tomato paste

1 onion, diced

1 carrot, diced

1 celery stalk, diced

3 garlic cloves, minced

4 cups no-salt-added
vegetable stock

2 cups water

1 cup red lentils

3 tablespoons lemon juice

¼ cup fresh
parsley, chopped

Red lentils are a great source of plant-based protein and fiber, making them a small but mighty member of the legume family. Lentils offer myriad nutrients, including magnesium, which can help reduce blood pressure and improve sleep quality. This soup gets extra flavor, texture, and bright acidity from the vegetables, spices, lemon juice, and parsley, making it a fantastic meal in a bowl.

1 Heat the olive oil in a large stock pot over medium-high heat. Add the cumin, coriander, turmeric, salt, and black pepper and cook, stirring, for 30 seconds. Add the tomato paste and cook, stirring, for 30 seconds to 1 minute. Add the onion, carrot, and celery and sauté 5 to 6 minutes. Add the garlic and sauté 30 seconds.

2 Add the vegetable stock, water, and lentils and bring to a boil. Turn down the heat to low, and simmer, covering partially, until the lentils are tender, about 20 minutes.

3 Mix in the lemon juice and parsley.

COOKING TIP: *To shorten prep time, look for precut mirepoix at your local grocery store. This is the appropriate mix of diced onion, carrot, and celery needed for the soup.*

Per Serving Calories: 170; Total fat: 3g; Saturated fat: 0g; Cholesterol: 0mg; Sodium: 340mg; Potassium: 455mg; Total Carbohydrates: 27g; Fiber: 6g; Sugars: 5g; Protein: 9g; Magnesium: 10mg; Calcium: 35mg

Tuscan Bean Soup with Kale

SERVES 4 ■ PREP TIME: 20 MINUTES ■ COOK TIME: 25 MINUTES

2 tablespoons extra-virgin olive oil

1 onion, diced

1 carrot, diced

1 celery stalk, diced

1 teaspoon kosher salt

4 cups no-salt-added vegetable stock

1 (15-ounce) can no-salt-added or low-sodium cannellini beans, drained and rinsed

1 tablespoon fresh thyme, chopped

1 tablespoon fresh sage, chopped

1 tablespoon fresh oregano, chopped

¼ teaspoon freshly ground black pepper

1 bunch kale, stemmed and chopped

¼ cup grated Parmesan cheese (optional)

Cannellini beans, also known as white kidney beans, make a hearty, nutritious base for soup. They have a subtle flavor, making them an excellent vehicle to absorb other flavors from the dressing, soup, or sauce in any dish. Adding kale to soup is a great way to get in more greens and bump up your vegetable intake. This soup works well with most hearty greens, so spinach, Swiss chard, mustard greens, or escarole all work and offer slightly different flavor profiles. The fresh herbs can be replaced with 1 teaspoon of each dried herb.

1 Heat the olive oil in a large pot over medium-high heat. Add the onion, carrot, celery, and salt and sauté until translucent and slightly golden, 5 to 6 minutes.

2 Add the vegetable stock, beans, thyme, sage, oregano, and black pepper and bring to a boil. Turn down the heat to low, and simmer for 10 minutes. Stir in the kale and let it wilt, about 5 minutes.

3 Sprinkle 1 tablespoon Parmesan cheese over each bowl before serving, if desired.

Per Serving Calories: 235; Total fat: 8g; Saturated fat: 1g; Cholesterol: 0mg; Sodium: 540mg; Potassium: 870mg; Total Carbohydrates: 35g; Fiber: 7g; Sugars: 6g; Protein: 9g; Magnesium: 105mg; Calcium: 205mg

Silky Tomato Soup

SERVES 4 ▪ PREP TIME: 20 MINUTES ▪ COOK TIME: 15 MINUTES

1 tablespoon extra-virgin
   olive oil

1 onion, diced

2 garlic cloves, sliced

1 tablespoon no-salt-added
   tomato paste

2 pounds
   tomatoes, chopped

½ cup no-salt-added
   vegetable stock

¾ cup fresh basil, chopped
   and divided

1 teaspoon kosher salt

¼ teaspoon freshly ground
   black pepper

8 ounces silken
   tofu, drained

1 cup cherry
   tomatoes, quartered

Standing in for the typical heavy cream, silken tofu provides creaminess and richness in this satisfying vegan soup. The tomatoes are chock-full of the antioxidant lycopene, which supports heart and bone health. And pairing cooked tomatoes with a fat like olive oil helps us better absorb lycopene.

1 Heat the olive oil in a large saucepan over medium-high heat. Add the onion and sauté until slightly golden, 5 to 6 minutes. Add the garlic and sauté for 30 seconds. Add the tomato paste and sauté for 30 seconds. Add the tomatoes and cook down a bit, 5 to 10 minutes. Add the stock, ½ cup of the basil, the salt, and black pepper.

2 Carefully transfer the mixture, in batches, to a high-powered blender or Vitamix. Add the tofu, and purée. Return the soup to the saucepan and simmer for 10 minutes.

3 Divide the cherry tomatoes among 4 bowls. Ladle the soup into the bowls. Garnish with the remaining ¼ cup basil.

COOKING TIP: *To make part of the soup ahead, complete step 1 and refrigerate for up to 5 days or freeze up to 3 months. Before serving, add the tofu and complete steps 2 and 3. This is a great way to enjoy the bounty of summer tomatoes when they're no longer in season.*

Per Serving Calories: 130; Total fat: 6g; Saturated fat: 1g; Cholesterol: 0mg; Sodium: 325mg; Potassium: 855mg; Total Carbohydrates: 17g; Fiber: 4g; Sugars: 10g; Protein: 6g; Magnesium: 55mg; Calcium: 70mg

Cauliflower Steaks with
Olive Citrus Sauce, page 84

CHAPTER 5
Vegetarian

Cauliflower Steaks with Olive Citrus Sauce

SERVES 4 ▪ PREP TIME: 15 MINUTES ▪ COOK TIME: 30 MINUTES

1 or 2 large heads cauliflower (at least 2 pounds, enough for 4 portions)

⅓ cup extra-virgin olive oil

¼ teaspoon kosher salt

⅛ teaspoon ground black pepper

Juice of 1 orange

Zest of 1 orange

¼ cup black olives, pitted and chopped

1 tablespoon Dijon or grainy mustard

1 tablespoon red wine vinegar

½ teaspoon ground coriander

Cauliflower steaks are a great alternative to, well, steak! A small list of ingredients with a big payoff, these cauliflower steaks are drizzled with olive oil, roasted in the oven to crispy tender perfection and are perfect as a vegan main entrée or side dish. Serve with this orange and olive sauce for a mouthwatering dinner. This dish pairs well with a bowl of Tuscan Bean Soup with Kale (page 80) or Pistachio Quinoa Salad with Pomegranate Citrus Vinaigrette (page 64). Once you've tasted cauliflower steaks, you'll never go back to steamed cauliflower again.

1 Preheat the oven to 400°F. Line a baking sheet with parchment paper or foil.

2 Cut off the stem of the cauliflower so it will sit upright. Slice it vertically into four thick slabs. Place the cauliflower on the prepared baking sheet. Drizzle with the olive oil, salt, and black pepper. Bake for about 30 minutes, turning over once, until tender and golden brown.

3 In a medium bowl, combine the orange juice, orange zest, olives, mustard, vinegar, and coriander; mix well.

4 Serve the cauliflower warm or at room temperature with the sauce.

Per Serving Calories: 265; Total fat: 21g; Saturated fat: 3g; Cholesterol: 0mg; Sodium: 310mg; Potassium: 810mg; Total Carbohydrates: 19g; Fiber: 4g; Sugars: 10g; Protein: 5g; Magnesium: 42mg; Calcium: 60mg

Pistachio Mint Pesto Pasta

SERVES 4 ▪ PREP TIME: 10 MINUTES ▪ COOK TIME: 10 MINUTES

8 ounces whole-
wheat pasta

1 cup fresh mint

½ cup fresh basil

⅓ cup unsalted
pistachios, shelled

1 garlic clove, peeled

½ teaspoon kosher salt

Juice of ½ lime

⅓ cup extra-virgin olive oil

Pistachio mint pesto is a unique twist on the classic pesto recipe, which contains basil, pine nuts, and Parmesan cheese. This version replaces the pine nuts with pistachios, eliminates the cheese, and adds mint. It's a cinch to make while the pasta cooks. I like to use whole-wheat penne or spaghetti, but feel free to use any pasta you like; it will all taste delicious. This versatile pesto also goes well on top of roasted vegetables, poultry, and fish.

1 Cook the pasta according to the package directions. Drain, reserving ½ cup of the pasta water, and set aside.

2 In a food processor, add the mint, basil, pistachios, garlic, salt, and lime juice. Process until the pistachios are coarsely ground. Add the olive oil in a slow, steady stream and process until incorporated.

3 In a large bowl, mix the pasta with the pistachio pesto; toss well to incorporate. If a thinner, more saucy consistency is desired, add some of the reserved pasta water and toss well.

VARIATION TIP: *Feel free to swap out the mint or basil for other herbs you have on hand. Parsley and cilantro work well and offer different flavor profiles that complement pasta, whole grains, or vegetables.*

Per Serving Calories: 420; Total fat: 3g; Saturated fat: 3g; Cholesterol: 0mg; Sodium: 150mg; Potassium: 290mg; Total Carbohydrates: 48g; Fiber: 2g; Sugars: 1g; Protein: 11g; Magnesium: 100mg; Calcium: 65mg

Burst Cherry Tomato Sauce with Angel Hair Pasta

SERVES 4 ▪ PREP TIME: 10 MINUTES ▪ COOK TIME: 20 MINUTES

8 ounces angel hair pasta

2 tablespoons extra-virgin olive oil

3 garlic cloves, minced

3 pints cherry tomatoes

½ teaspoon kosher salt

¼ teaspoon red pepper flakes

¾ cup fresh basil, chopped

1 tablespoon white balsamic vinegar (optional)

¼ cup grated Parmesan cheese (optional)

This one is for tomato lovers. Cherry tomatoes are readily available year-round, making them a go-to shopping cart staple. The sweet flavor of this simple sauce is balanced by the salty Parmesan cheese topping and ready by the time the pasta cooks. Get in some greens by adding a couple handfuls of chopped kale or Swiss chard to the pasta pot a few minutes before it's done, then drain all together.

1 Cook the pasta according to the package directions. Drain and set aside.

2 Heat the olive oil in a skillet or large sauté pan over medium-high heat. Add the garlic and sauté for 30 seconds. Add the tomatoes, salt, and red pepper flakes and cook, stirring occasionally, until the tomatoes burst, about 15 minutes.

3 Remove from the heat and add the pasta and basil. Toss together well. (For out-of-season tomatoes, add the vinegar, if desired, and mix well.)

4 Serve with the grated Parmesan cheese, if desired.

Per Serving Calories: 305; Total fat: 8g; Saturated fat: 1g; Cholesterol: 0mg; Sodium: 155mg; Potassium: 690mg; Total Carbohydrates: 53g; Fiber: 3g; Sugars: 7g; Protein: 11g; Magnesium: 112mg; Calcium: 65mg

Baked Tofu with Sun-Dried Tomatoes and Artichokes

SERVES 4 ▪ PREP TIME: 15 MINUTES, PLUS 15 MINUTES TO MARINATE
COOK TIME: 30 MINUTES

- 1 (16-ounce) package extra-firm tofu, drained and patted dry, cut into 1-inch cubes
- 2 tablespoons extra-virgin olive oil, divided
- 2 tablespoons lemon juice, divided
- 1 tablespoon low-sodium soy sauce or gluten-free tamari
- 1 onion, diced
- ½ teaspoon kosher salt
- 2 garlic cloves, minced
- 1 (14-ounce) can artichoke hearts, drained
- 8 sun-dried tomato halves packed in oil, drained and chopped
- ¼ teaspoon freshly ground black pepper
- 1 tablespoon white wine vinegar
- Zest of 1 lemon
- ¼ cup fresh parsley, chopped

Tofu is a high-quality source of plant-based protein, B vitamins, and iron. It has a super-mild flavor that adopts whatever seasonings you add, and marinating the tofu prior to cooking allows it to absorb more flavor, adding depth to the overall dish. Look for extra-firm tofu, which holds up well when baked, sautéed, or grilled.

1 Preheat the oven to 400°F. Line a baking sheet with foil or parchment paper.

2 In a bowl, combine the tofu, 1 tablespoon of the olive oil, 1 tablespoon of the lemon juice, and the soy sauce. Allow to sit and marinate for 15 to 30 minutes. Arrange the tofu in a single layer on the prepared baking sheet and bake for 20 minutes, turning once, until light golden brown.

3 Heat the remaining 1 tablespoon olive oil in a large skillet or sauté pan over medium heat. Add the onion and salt; sauté until translucent, 5 to 6 minutes. Add the garlic and sauté for 30 seconds. Add the artichoke hearts, sun-dried tomatoes, and black pepper and sauté for 5 minutes. Add the white wine vinegar and the remaining 1 tablespoon lemon juice and deglaze the pan, scraping up any brown bits. Remove the pan from the heat and stir in the lemon zest and parsley. Gently mix in the baked tofu.

Per Serving Calories: 230; Total fat: 14g; Saturated fat: 2g; Cholesterol: 0mg; Sodium: 500mg; Potassium: 220mg; Total Carbohydrates: 13g; Fiber: 5g; Sugars: 3g; Protein: 14g; Magnesium: 13mg; Calcium: 110mg

Baked Mediterranean Tempeh with Tomatoes and Garlic

SERVES 4 ▪ PREP TIME: 25 MINUTES, PLUS 4 HOURS TO MARINATE
COOK TIME: 35 MINUTES

FOR THE TEMPEH

12 ounces tempeh

¼ cup white wine

2 tablespoons extra-virgin
olive oil

2 tablespoons lemon juice

Zest of 1 lemon

¼ teaspoon kosher salt

¼ teaspoon freshly ground
black pepper

**FOR THE TOMATOES AND
GARLIC SAUCE**

1 tablespoon extra-virgin
olive oil

1 onion, diced

3 garlic cloves, minced

1 (14.5-ounce) can no-salt-
added crushed tomatoes

1 beefsteak tomato, diced

1 dried bay leaf

1 teaspoon white
wine vinegar

1 teaspoon lemon juice

1 teaspoon dried oregano

1 teaspoon dried thyme

¾ teaspoon kosher salt

¼ cup basil, cut into ribbons

New to tempeh? Though not as well-known as tofu, it is a mainstay of many vegetarian and vegan diets and a complete protein on its own. Tempeh is a soy-based product, made from fermented cooked soybeans and often combined with other beans and grains, then pressed into a firm, dense cake—soy-free versions are available if preferred. I suggest simmering or steaming the tempeh prior to marinating to remove the slightly bitter flavor that is sometimes present. Simmering also makes it softer and more porous, so that it can better absorb marinade. This delicious Mediterranean-style tempeh can be enjoyed on its own or served over brown rice with a side of Green Beans with Pine Nuts and Garlic (page 46).

TO MAKE THE TEMPEH

1 Place the tempeh in a medium saucepan. Add enough water to cover it by 1 to 2 inches. Bring to a boil over medim-high heat, cover, and lower heat to a simmer. Cook for 10 to 15 minutes. Remove the tempeh, pat dry, cool, and cut into 1-inch cubes.

2 In a large bowl, combine the white wine, olive oil, lemon juice, lemon zest, salt, and black pepper. Add the tempeh, cover the bowl, and put in the refrigerator for 4 hours, or up to overnight.

3 Preheat the oven to 375°F. Place the marinated tempeh and the marinade in a baking dish and cook for 15 minutes.

TO MAKE THE TOMATOES AND GARLIC SAUCE

4 Heat the olive oil in a large skillet over medium heat. Add the onion and sauté until transparent, 3 to 5 minutes. Add the garlic and sauté for 30 seconds. Add the crushed tomatoes, beefsteak tomato, bay leaf, vinegar, lemon juice, oregano, thyme, and salt. Mix well. Simmer for 15 minutes.

5 Add the baked tempeh to the tomato mixture and gently mix together. Garnish with the basil.

SUBSTITUTION TIP: *If you're out of tempeh or simply want to speed up the cooking process, you can swap in a 14.5-ounce can of white beans for the tempeh. Drain and rinse the beans and add them to the sauce with the crushed tomatoes. It still makes a great vegan entrée in half the time!*

Per Serving Calories: 330; Total fat: 20g; Saturated fat: 3g; Cholesterol: 0mg; Sodium: 305mg; Potassium: 865mg; Total Carbohydrates: 22g; Fiber: 4g; Sugars: 6g; Protein: 18g; Magnesium: 82mg; Calcium: 125mg

Roasted Portobello Mushrooms with Kale and Red Onion

SERVES 4 ■ PREP TIME: 15 MINUTES, PLUS 15 MINUTES TO MARINATE
COOK TIME: 30 MINUTES

¼ cup white wine vinegar

3 tablespoons extra-virgin olive oil, divided

½ teaspoon honey

¾ teaspoon kosher salt, divided

¼ teaspoon freshly ground black pepper

4 large (4 to 5 ounces each) portobello mushrooms, stems removed

1 red onion, julienned

2 garlic cloves, minced

1 (8-ounce) bunch kale, stemmed and chopped small

¼ teaspoon red pepper flakes

¼ cup grated Parmesan or Romano cheese

I love the meatiness of a roasted portobello mushroom. One of the best things about them, aside from their delicious flavor, is their size. Because of their burger-like size and shape, making stuffed portobellos is a breeze. These portobellos are marinated, roasted, stuffed with sautéed kale, topped with cheese, and broiled to perfection. They work well as a vegetarian entrée, side dish, or appetizer. And here's a little secret—this is one of my favorite recipes in the whole book!

1 Line a baking sheet with parchment paper or foil. In a medium bowl, whisk together the vinegar, 1½ tablespoons of the olive oil, honey, ¼ teaspoon of the salt, and the black pepper. Arrange the mushrooms on the baking sheet and pour the marinade over them. Marinate for 15 to 30 minutes.

2 Meanwhile, preheat the oven to 400°F.

3 Bake the mushrooms for 20 minutes, turning over halfway through.

4 Heat the remaining 1½ tablespoons olive oil in a large skillet or ovenproof sauté pan over medium-high heat. Add the onion and the remaining ½ teaspoon salt and sauté until golden brown, 5 to 6 minutes. Add the garlic and sauté for 30 seconds. Add the kale and red pepper flakes and sauté until the kale cooks down, about 5 minutes.

5 Remove the mushrooms from the oven and increase the temperature to broil.

6 Carefully pour the liquid from the baking sheet into the pan with the kale mixture; mix well.

7 Turn the mushrooms over so that the stem side is facing up. Spoon some of the kale mixture on top of each mushroom. Sprinkle 1 tablespoon Parmesan cheese on top of each.

8 Broil until golden brown, 3 to 4 minutes.

Per Serving Calories: 200; Total fat: 13g; Saturated fat: 3g; Cholesterol: 6mg; Sodium: 365mg; Potassium: 860mg; Total Carbohydrates: 16g; Fiber: 4g; Sugars: 6g; Protein: 8g; Magnesium: 60mg; Calcium: 210mg

Balsamic Marinated Tofu with Basil and Oregano

SERVES 4 ▪ PREP TIME: 10 MINUTES, PLUS 30 MINUTES TO MARINATE
COOK TIME: 30 MINUTES

¼ cup extra-virgin olive oil

¼ cup balsamic vinegar

2 tablespoons low-sodium soy sauce or gluten-free tamari

3 garlic cloves, grated

2 teaspoons pure maple syrup

Zest of 1 lemon

1 teaspoon dried basil

1 teaspoon dried oregano

½ teaspoon dried thyme

½ teaspoon dried sage

¼ teaspoon kosher salt

¼ teaspoon freshly ground black pepper

¼ teaspoon red pepper flakes (optional)

1 (16-ounce) block extra firm tofu, drained and patted dry, cut into ½-inch or 1-inch cubes

This marinated and baked tofu recipe is my favorite way to enjoy tofu: crispy outside, tender inside, and layered with flavor. You can also eat it as a snack, add it to salads, or mix it into a bowl with whole grains. Look for tofu in the refrigerated section of grocery stores, either in the produce section, near the cheese section, or in the health food area.

1 In a bowl or gallon zip-top bag, mix together the olive oil, vinegar, soy sauce, garlic, maple syrup, lemon zest, basil, oregano, thyme, sage, salt, black pepper, and red pepper flakes, if desired. Add the tofu and mix gently. Put in the refrigerator and marinate for 30 minutes, or up to overnight if you desire.

2 Preheat the oven to 425°F. Line a baking sheet with parchment paper or foil. Arrange the marinated tofu in a single layer on the prepared baking sheet. Bake for 20 to 30 minutes, turning over halfway through, until slightly crispy on the outside and tender on the inside.

Per Serving Calories: 225; Total fat: 16g; Saturated fat: 2g; Cholesterol: 0mg; Sodium: 265mg; Potassium: 65mg; Total Carbohydrates: 9g; Fiber: 2g; Sugars: 5g; Protein: 13g; Magnesium: 6mg; Calcium: 112mg

Ricotta, Basil, and Pistachio-Stuffed Zucchini

SERVES 4 ● PREP TIME: 15 MINUTES ● COOK TIME: 25 MINUTES

2 medium zucchini,
    halved lengthwise

1 tablespoon extra-virgin
    olive oil

1 onion, diced

1 teaspoon kosher salt

2 garlic cloves, minced

¾ cup ricotta cheese

¼ cup unsalted pistachios,
    shelled and chopped

¼ cup fresh basil, chopped

1 large egg, beaten

¼ teaspoon freshly ground
    black pepper

These stuffed zucchini "boats" are baked and filled with a lemon ricotta. This dish is especially lovely in the summer when zucchini is bountiful and overflowing in gardens and at farmers' markets. Try this recipe as a vegetarian main course or as a side dish. For a little twist, add chopped tomatoes in step 3.

1 Preheat the oven to 425°F. Line a baking sheet with parchment paper or foil.

2 Scoop out the seeds/pulp from the zucchini, leaving ¼-inch flesh around the edges. Transfer the pulp to a cutting board and chop the pulp.

3 Heat the olive oil in a large skillet or sauté pan over medium heat. Add the onion, pulp, and salt and sauté about 5 minutes. Add the garlic and sauté 30 seconds.

4 In a medium bowl, combine the ricotta cheese, pistachios, basil, egg, and black pepper. Add the onion mixture and mix together well.

5 Place the 4 zucchini halves on the prepared baking sheet. Fill the zucchini halves with the ricotta mixture. Bake for 20 minutes, or until golden brown.

Per Serving Calories: 200; Total fat: 12g; Saturated fat: 4g; Cholesterol: 61mg; Sodium: 360mg; Potassium: 650mg; Total Carbohydrates: 14g; Fiber: 3g; Sugars: 7g; Protein: 11g; Magnesium: 52mg; Calcium: 185mg

Farro with Roasted Tomatoes and Mushrooms

SERVES 4 AS A MAIN OR 6 AS A SIDE ▪ PREP TIME: 20 MINUTES ▪ COOK TIME: 1 HOUR

FOR THE TOMATOES

2 pints cherry tomatoes

1 teaspoon extra-virgin
olive oil

¼ teaspoon kosher salt

FOR THE FARRO

3 to 4 cups water

½ cup farro

¼ teaspoon kosher salt

FOR THE MUSHROOMS

2 tablespoons extra-virgin
olive oil

1 onion, julienned

½ teaspoon kosher salt

¼ teaspoon freshly ground
black pepper

10 ounces baby bella
(crimini) mushrooms,
stemmed and sliced thin

½ cup no-salt-added
vegetable stock

1 (15-ounce) can no-salt-
added or low-sodium
cannellini beans, drained
and rinsed

1 cup baby spinach

2 tablespoons fresh basil,
cut into ribbons

¼ cup pine nuts, toasted

Aged balsamic vinegar
(optional)

Farro is an ancient grain and a wild cousin of wheat. It is packed with plant-based protein and fiber, which helps reduce inflammation and promotes heart health. It looks like large puffed rice when cooked and has a slightly nutty taste and a chewy, al dente texture. Look for it in the grain or bulk area at your local grocery store. To make this recipe gluten-free, swap out the farro for quinoa, brown rice, or sorghum.

TO MAKE THE TOMATOES

Preheat the oven to 400°F. Line a baking sheet with parchment paper or foil. Toss the tomatoes, olive oil, and salt together on the baking sheet and roast for 30 minutes.

TO MAKE THE FARRO

Bring the water, farro, and salt to a boil in a medium saucepan or pot over high heat. Cover, reduce the heat to low, and simmer, and cook for 30 minutes, or until the farro is al dente. Drain and set aside.

TO MAKE THE MUSHROOMS

1 Heat the olive oil in a large skillet or sauté pan over medium-low heat. Add the onions, salt, and black pepper and sauté until golden brown and starting to caramelize, about 15 minutes. Add the mushrooms, increase the heat to medium, and sauté until the liquid has evaporated and the mushrooms brown, about 10 minutes. Add the vegetable stock and deglaze the pan, scraping up any brown bits, and reduce the liquid for about 5 minutes. Add the beans and warm through, about 3 minutes.

2 Remove from the heat and mix in the spinach, basil, pine nuts, roasted tomatoes, and farro. Garnish with a drizzle of balsamic vinegar, if desired.

Per Serving Calories: 375; Total fat: 15g; Saturated fat: 2g; Cholesterol: 0mg; Sodium: 305mg; Potassium: 1,050mg; Total Carbohydrates: 48g; Fiber: 10g; Sugars: 8g; Protein: 14g; Magnesium: 110mg; Calcium: 100mg

Baked Orzo with Eggplant, Swiss Chard, and Mozzarella

SERVES 4 AS A MAIN OR 6 AS A SIDE ▪ PREP TIME: 20 MINUTES ▪ COOK TIME: 1 HOUR

- 2 tablespoons extra-virgin olive oil
- 1 large (1-pound) eggplant, diced small
- 2 carrots, peeled and diced small
- 2 celery stalks, diced small
- 1 onion, diced small
- ½ teaspoon kosher salt
- 3 garlic cloves, minced
- ¼ teaspoon freshly ground black pepper
- 1 cup whole-wheat orzo
- 1 teaspoon no-salt-added tomato paste
- 1½ cups no-salt-added vegetable stock
- 1 cup Swiss chard, stemmed and chopped small
- 2 tablespoons fresh oregano, chopped
- Zest of 1 lemon
- 4 ounces mozzarella cheese, diced small
- ¼ cup grated Parmesan cheese
- 2 tomatoes, sliced ½-inch-thick

Most pasta recipes begin with boiling a pot of water. Here's your chance to skip that step. Instead, we combine a variety of vegetables with orzo and vegetable stock, throw in some cheese, and bake the entire thing. To keep it a one-pot dish, I recommend a large oven-safe sauté pan with high sides. If you don't have one, simply transfer all the ingredients into a large baking dish in step 3. I like using whole-wheat orzo, but regular orzo also works well.

1 Preheat the oven to 400°F.

2 Heat the olive oil in a large oven-safe sauté pan over medium heat. Add the eggplant, carrots, celery, onion, and salt and sauté about 10 minutes. Add the garlic and black pepper and sauté about 30 seconds. Add the orzo and tomato paste and sauté 1 minute. Add the vegetable stock and deglaze the pan, scraping up the brown bits. Add the Swiss chard, oregano, and lemon zest and stir until the chard wilts.

3 Remove from the heat and mix in the mozzarella cheese. Smooth the top of the orzo mixture flat. Sprinkle the Parmesan cheese over the top. Arrange the tomatoes in a single layer on top of the Parmesan cheese. Bake for 45 minutes.

Per Serving Calories: 470; Total fat: 17g; Saturated fat: 6g; Cholesterol: 28mg; Sodium: 545mg; Potassium: 770mg; Total Carbohydrates: 65g; Fiber: 7g; Sugars: 13g; Protein: 18g; Magnesium: 53mg; Calcium: 270mg

Barley Risotto with Tomatoes

SERVES 4 ▪ PREP TIME: 20 MINUTES ▪ COOK TIME: 45 MINUTES

2 tablespoons extra-virgin
    olive oil

2 celery stalks, diced

½ cup shallots, diced

4 garlic cloves, minced

3 cups no-salt-added
    vegetable stock

1 (14.5-ounce) can no-salt-
    added diced tomatoes

1 (14.5-ounce) can no-salt-
    added crushed tomatoes

1 cup pearl barley

Zest of 1 lemon

1 teaspoon kosher salt

½ teaspoon smoked paprika

¼ teaspoon red
    pepper flakes

¼ teaspoon freshly ground
    black pepper

4 thyme sprigs

1 dried bay leaf

2 cups baby spinach

½ cup crumbled
    feta cheese

1 tablespoon fresh
    oregano, chopped

1 tablespoon fennel seeds,
    toasted (optional)

Pearl barley steps in for arborio rice in this hearty vegetarian risotto. Similar to arborio, barley cooks slowly and creates a creamy texture as it softens. This dish is packed with vegetables and seasoned with a variety of herbs and spices. The smoked paprika adds an aromatic, smoky flavor to the dish, but if you're not a fan of smoky, no problem! Sweet paprika can be used just as easily—or feel free to leave it out of the dish entirely. For a gluten-free version, use pearled sorghum instead of barley.

1 Heat the olive oil in a large saucepan over medium heat. Add the celery and shallots and sauté, about 4 to 5 minutes. Add the garlic and sauté 30 seconds. Add the vegetable stock, diced tomatoes, crushed tomatoes, barley, lemon zest, salt, paprika, red pepper flakes, black pepper, thyme, and the bay leaf, and mix well. Bring to a boil, then lower to low, and simmer. Cook, stirring occasionally, for 40 minutes.

2 Remove the bay leaf and thyme sprigs. Stir in the spinach.

3 In a small bowl, combine the feta, oregano, and fennel seeds. Serve the barley risotto in bowls topped with the feta mixture.

Per Serving Calories: 375; Total fat: 12g; Saturated fat: 4g; Cholesterol: 17mg; Sodium: 570mg; Potassium: 850mg; Total Carbohydrates: 57g; Fiber: 13g; Sugars: 11g; Protein: 11g; Magnesium: 90mg; Calcium: 210mg

Chickpeas and Kale with Spicy Pomodoro Sauce

SERVES 4 ▪ PREP TIME: 10 MINUTES ▪ COOK TIME: 35 MINUTES

2 tablespoons extra-virgin olive oil

4 garlic cloves, sliced

1 teaspoon red pepper flakes

1 (28-ounce) can no-salt-added crushed tomatoes

1 teaspoon kosher salt

½ teaspoon honey

1 bunch kale, stemmed and chopped

2 (15-ounce) cans no-salt-added or low-sodium chickpeas, drained and rinsed

¼ cup fresh basil, chopped

¼ cup grated pecorino Romano cheese

Pomodoro sauce is a thicker, smoother version of marinara that often has a deeper, darker red hue. I recommend simmering and reducing the sauce for 20 minutes, but you can definitely cook it longer if you like. Adding the red pepper flakes directly to the oil infuses the dish with spiciness throughout. If you prefer a less spicy version, simply add the red pepper flakes at the end in step 3. For an extra nutrient boost, serve this dish over zucchini noodles.

1 Heat the olive oil in a large skillet or sauté pan over medium heat. Add the garlic and red pepper flakes and sauté until the garlic is a light golden brown, about 2 minutes. Add the tomatoes, salt, and honey and mix well. Reduce the heat to low and simmer for 20 minutes.

2 Add the kale and mix in well. Cook about 5 minutes. Add the chickpeas and simmer about 5 minutes.

3 Remove from heat and stir in the basil. Serve topped with pecorino cheese.

Per Serving Calories: 420; Total fat: 13g; Saturated fat: 4g; Cholesterol: 15mg; Sodium: 570mg; Potassium: 1,250mg; Total Carbohydrates: 54g; Fiber: 12g; Sugars: 9g; Protein: 20g; Magnesium: 175mg; Calcium: 440mg

Roasted Feta with Kale and Lemon Yogurt

SERVES 4 ▪ PREP TIME: 15 MINUTES ▪ COOK TIME: 20 MINUTES

1 tablespoon extra-virgin
   olive oil

1 onion, julienned

¼ teaspoon kosher salt

1 teaspoon ground turmeric

½ teaspoon ground cumin

½ teaspoon
   ground coriander

¼ teaspoon freshly ground
   black pepper

1 bunch kale, stemmed
   and chopped

7-ounce block feta cheese,
   cut into ¼-inch-thick
   slices

½ cup plain Greek yogurt

1 tablespoon lemon juice

There are several varieties of kale—some curly, some flat, some dark green, and others with more of a red, blue, or purple hue—but all become tender when cooked. Kale is a nutrient powerhouse, loaded with calcium, fiber, and vitamin K, to name a few. It is easily found year-round and stores well for up to a week in the crisper drawer if kept in a bunch and wrapped with paper towels. To take this dish to the next level, I recommend serving it with Roasted Za'atar Chickpeas (page 59). The crunchy chickpeas add texture to the dish, pairing beautifully with the tender cooked kale, creamy feta cheese, and lemony yogurt.

1 Preheat the oven to 400°F.

2 Heat the olive oil in a large ovenproof skillet or sauté pan over medium heat. Add the onion and salt; sauté until lightly golden brown, about 5 minutes. Add the turmeric, cumin, coriander, and black pepper; sauté for 30 seconds. Add the kale and sauté about 2 minutes. Add ½ cup water and continue to cook down the kale, about 3 minutes.

3 Remove from the heat and place the feta cheese slices on top of the kale mixture. Place in the oven and bake until the feta softens, 10 to 12 minutes.

4 In a small bowl, combine the yogurt and lemon juice.

5 Serve the kale and feta cheese topped with the lemon yogurt.

Per Serving Calories: 210; Total fat: 14g; Saturated fat: 8g; Cholesterol: 44mg; Sodium: 565mg; Potassium: 340mg; Total Carbohydrates: 11g; Fiber: 2g; Sugars: 5g; Protein: 11g; Magnesium: 55mg; Calcium: 375mg

Roasted Eggplant and Chickpeas with Tomato Sauce

SERVES 4 ▪ PREP TIME: 15 MINUTES ▪ COOK TIME: 1 HOUR

Olive oil cooking spray

1 large (about 1 pound) eggplant, sliced into ¼-inch-thick rounds

1 teaspoon kosher salt, divided

1 tablespoon extra-virgin olive oil

3 garlic cloves, minced

1 (28-ounce) can no-salt-added crushed tomatoes

½ teaspoon honey

¼ teaspoon freshly ground black pepper

2 tablespoons fresh basil, chopped

1 (15-ounce) can no-salt-added or low-sodium chickpeas, drained and rinsed

¾ cup crumbled feta cheese

1 tablespoon fresh oregano, chopped

This hearty, vegetarian dish is a healthy variation on eggplant Parmesan. The casserole is made up of layers of chickpeas, roasted eggplant, homemade marinara sauce, and feta cheese, and baked until bubbly. Serve with Roasted Harissa Carrots (page 47) and sautéed asparagus.

1 Preheat the oven to 425°F. Line two baking sheets with foil and lightly spray with olive oil cooking spray. Arrange the eggplant in a single layer and sprinkle with ½ teaspoon of the salt. Bake for 20 minutes, turning once halfway, until lightly golden brown.

2 Meanwhile, heat the olive oil in a large saucepan over medium heat. Add the garlic and sauté for 30 seconds. Add the crushed tomatoes, honey, the remaining ½ teaspoon salt, and black pepper. Simmer about 20 minutes, until the sauce reduces a bit and thickens. Stir in the basil.

3 After removing the eggplant from the oven, reduce the oven temperature to 375°F. In a large rectangular or oval baking dish, ladle in the chickpeas and 1 cup sauce. Layer the eggplant slices on top, overlapping as necessary to cover the chickpeas. Spread the remaining sauce on top of the eggplant. Sprinkle the feta cheese and oregano on top.

4 Cover the baking dish with foil and bake for 15 minutes. Remove the foil and bake an additional 15 minutes.

Per Serving Calories: 320; Total fat: 11g; Saturated fat: 5g; Cholesterol: 25mg; Sodium: 565mg; Potassium: 1,120mg; Total Carbohydrates: 40g; Fiber: 12g; Sugars: 14g; Protein: 14g; Magnesium: 110mg; Calcium: 275mg

Baked Falafel Sliders

MAKES 6 SLIDERS ▪ PREP TIME: 10 MINUTES ▪ COOK TIME: 30 MINUTES

Olive oil cooking spray

1 (15-ounce) can no-salt-added or low-sodium chickpeas, drained and rinsed

1 onion, roughly chopped

2 garlic cloves, peeled

2 tablespoons fresh parsley, chopped

2 tablespoons whole-wheat flour

½ teaspoon ground coriander

½ teaspoon ground cumin

½ teaspoon baking powder

½ teaspoon kosher salt

¼ teaspoon freshly ground black pepper

Falafel is a popular vegan dish often regarded as "fast food" and sold by street vendors. It is typically deep fried and served stuffed in a pita with lettuce, tomatoes, and hummus, or on top of a salad. We skip the deep frying here by forming small patties and baking them. To make this recipe gluten-free, use a gluten-free flour such as sorghum or chickpea flour. I love to serve these sliders on a bed of greens with a whole-wheat pita, sliced tomatoes, and Tzatziki (page 151) on the side.

1 Preheat the oven to 350°F. Line a baking sheet with parchment paper or foil and lightly spray with olive oil cooking spray.

2 In a food processor, add the chickpeas, onion, garlic, parsley, flour, coriander, cumin, baking powder, salt, and black pepper. Process until smooth, stopping to scrape down the sides of the bowl.

3 Make 6 slider patties, each with a heaping ¼ cup of mixture, and arrange on the prepared baking sheet. Bake for 30 minutes, turning over halfway through.

Per Serving (1 slider) Calories: 90; Total fat: 1g; Saturated fat: 0g; Cholesterol: 0mg; Sodium: 110mg; Potassium: 230mg; Total Carbohydrates: 17g; Fiber: 3g; Sugars: 1g; Protein: 4g; Magnesium: 28mg; Calcium: 62mg

Quinoa Lentil "Meatballs" with Quick Tomato Sauce

SERVES 4 ▪ PREP TIME: 25 MINUTES ▪ COOK TIME: 45 MINUTES

FOR THE MEATBALLS

Olive oil cooking spray

2 large eggs, beaten

1 tablespoon no-salt-added tomato paste

½ teaspoon kosher salt

½ cup grated Parmesan cheese

½ onion, roughly chopped

¼ cup fresh parsley

1 garlic clove, peeled

1½ cups cooked lentils

1 cup cooked quinoa

FOR THE TOMATO SAUCE

1 tablespoon extra-virgin olive oil

1 onion, minced

½ teaspoon dried oregano

½ teaspoon kosher salt

2 garlic cloves, minced

1 (28-ounce) can no-salt-added crushed tomatoes

½ teaspoon honey

¼ cup fresh basil, chopped

These "meatballs" are terrific served on their own or over zucchini noodles as a vegetarian main, or as a delicious appetizer for more than four people. If you have no time to cook dry lentils, use a 14.5-ounce can of lentils, drained and rinsed. Leftover quinoa or precooked quinoa (shelf stable or thawed if frozen) also works well if you're looking for another prep shortcut. This is a great make-ahead dish. Cook a double batch of the recipe and store leftovers in the freezer for up to 3 months.

TO MAKE THE MEATBALLS

1 Preheat the oven to 400°F. Lightly grease a 12-cup muffin pan with olive oil cooking spray.

2 In a large bowl, whisk together the eggs, tomato paste, and salt until fully combined. Mix in the Parmesan cheese.

3 In a food processor, add the onion, parsley, and garlic. Process until minced. Add to the egg mixture and stir together. Add the lentils to the food processor and process until puréed into a thick paste. Add to the large bowl and mix together. Add the quinoa and mix well.

4 Form balls, slightly larger than a golf ball, with ¼ cup of the quinoa mixture. Place each ball in a muffin pan cup. Note: The mixture will be somewhat soft but should hold together.

5 Bake 25 to 30 minutes, until golden brown.

TO MAKE THE TOMATO SAUCE

6 Heat the olive oil in a large saucepan over medium heat. Add the onion, oregano, and salt and sauté until light golden brown, about 5 minutes. Add the garlic and cook for 30 seconds.

7 Stir in the tomatoes and honey. Increase the heat to high and cook, stirring often, until simmering, then decrease the heat to medium-low and cook for 10 minutes. Remove from the heat and stir in the basil. Serve with the meatballs.

VARIATION TIP: *If you prefer a sweet and spicy sauce, add ½ teaspoon red pepper flakes to the tomato sauce when adding the salt.*

Per Serving (3 meatballs and ¾ cup sauce) Calories: 360; Total fat: 10g; Saturated fat: 3g; Cholesterol: 100mg; Sodium: 520mg; Potassium: 1,185mg; Total Carbohydrates: 48g; Fiber: 14g; Sugars: 12g; Protein: 20g; Magnesium: 75mg; Calcium: 190mg

**Grilled Mahi-Mahi with
Artichoke Caponata, page 111**

CHAPTER 6
Fish and Shellfish

Citrus-Glazed Salmon with Zucchini Noodles

SERVES 4 ■ PREP TIME: 10 MINUTES ■ COOK TIME: 20 MINUTES

4 (5- to 6-ounce) pieces salmon

½ teaspoon kosher salt

¼ teaspoon freshly ground black pepper

1 tablespoon extra-virgin olive oil

1 cup freshly squeezed orange juice

1 teaspoon low-sodium soy sauce

2 zucchini (about 16 ounces), spiralized

1 tablespoon fresh chives, chopped

1 tablespoon fresh parsley, chopped

These pan-seared salmon fillets are glazed with a tasty citrus sauce and served over zucchini noodles for an extra boost of nutrients. Don't have a spiralizer? Most grocery stores carry prespiralized vegetables in the produce area. If zucchini isn't your thing, feel free to try out other vegetable noodles; carrots would also go well in this dish.

1 Preheat the oven to 350°F. Season the salmon with salt and black pepper.

2 Heat the olive oil in a large oven-safe skillet or sauté pan over medium-high heat. Add the salmon, skin-side down, and sear for 5 minutes, or until the skin is golden brown and crispy. Turn the salmon over and transfer to the oven until your desired doneness is reached—about 5 minutes for medium-rare, 7 minutes for medium, and 9 minutes for medium-well. Place the salmon on a cutting board to rest.

3 Place the same pan on the stove over medium-high heat. Add the orange juice and soy sauce to deglaze the pan. Bring to a simmer, scraping up any brown bits, and continue to simmer 5 to 7 minutes, until the liquid is reduced by half to a syrup-like consistency.

4 Divide the zucchini noodles among 4 plates and place 1 piece of salmon on each. Pour the orange glaze over the salmon and zucchini noodles. Garnish with the chives and parsley.

SUBSTITUTION TIP: *Arctic char is a great substitute for the salmon.*

VARIATION TIP: *I prefer to keep my zucchini noodles raw when placing hot food on them, which will, in turn, warm them up and keep them intact. But you can also sauté the zucchini noodles prior to plating them. To do this, heat oil in a sauté pan over medium-high heat, and sauté the zucchini noodles for 2 to 3 minutes.*

Per Serving Calories: 280 Total fat: 13g; Saturated fat: 2g; Cholesterol: 78mg; Sodium: 255mg; Potassium: 1100mg; Total Carbohydrates: 11g; Fiber: 1g; Sugars: 8g; Protein: 30g; Magnesium: 70mg; Calcium: 45mg

Salmon Cakes with Bell Pepper and Lemon Yogurt

SERVES 4 ▪ PREP TIME: 15 MINUTES ▪ COOK TIME: 15 MINUTES

¼ cup whole-wheat bread crumbs

¼ cup mayonnaise

1 large egg, beaten

1 tablespoon chives, chopped

1 tablespoon fresh parsley, chopped

Zest of 1 lemon

¾ teaspoon kosher salt, divided

¼ teaspoon freshly ground black pepper

2 (5- to 6-ounce) cans no-salt boneless/skinless salmon, drained and finely flaked

½ bell pepper, diced small

2 tablespoons extra-virgin olive oil, divided

1 cup plain Greek yogurt

Juice of 1 lemon

These delicious salmon cakes are a unique play on the traditional crab cake recipe and an easy way to get in those heart-healthy omega-3 fatty acids! In addition, canned salmon is one of the best sources of nondairy calcium available. Panfrying the cakes creates a crispy texture outside while remaining soft on the inside. Serve with Green Beans with Pine Nuts and Garlic (page 46) or Roasted Cauliflower and Arugula Salad with Pomegranate and Pine Nuts (page 75).

1 In a large bowl, combine the bread crumbs, mayonnaise, egg, chives, parsley, lemon zest, ½ teaspoon of the salt, and black pepper and mix well. Add the salmon and the bell pepper and stir gently until well combined. Shape the mixture into 8 patties.

2 Heat 1 tablespoon of the olive oil in a large skillet over medium-high heat. Cook half the cakes until the bottoms are golden brown, 4 to 5 minutes. Adjust the heat to medium if the bottoms start to burn. Flip the cakes and cook until golden brown, an additional 4 to 5 minutes. Repeat with the remaining 1 tablespoon olive oil and the rest of the cakes.

3 In a small bowl, combine the yogurt, lemon juice, and the remaining ¼ teaspoon salt and mix well. Serve with the salmon cakes.

Per Serving Calories: 330; Total fat: 23g; Saturated fat: 4g; Cholesterol: 91mg; Sodium: 385mg; Potassium: 135mg; Total Carbohydrates: 9g; Fiber: 1g; Sugars: 3g; Protein: 21g; Magnesium: 10mg; Calcium: 65mg

Halibut in Parchment with Zucchini, Shallots, and Herbs

SERVES 4 ▪ PREP TIME: 15 MINUTES ▪ COOK TIME: 15 MINUTES

½ cup zucchini, diced small

1 shallot, minced

4 (5-ounce) halibut fillets (about 1 inch thick)

4 teaspoons extra-virgin olive oil

¼ teaspoon kosher salt

⅛ teaspoon freshly ground black pepper

1 lemon, sliced into ⅛-inch-thick rounds

8 sprigs of thyme

This dish comes together quickly with minimal prep and cooking time. Using parchment paper helps steam the fish and retain moisture. I recommend serving the saucy contents of the packet over brown rice to help soak up the juices. No parchment paper? Foil works just as well.

1 Preheat the oven to 450°F. Combine the zucchini and shallots in a medium bowl.

2 Cut 4 (15-by-24-inch) pieces of parchment paper. Fold each sheet in half horizontally. Draw a large half heart on one side of each folded sheet, with the fold along the center of the heart. Cut out the heart, open the parchment, and lay it flat.

3 Place a fillet near the center of each parchment heart. Drizzle 1 teaspoon olive oil on each fillet. Sprinkle with salt and pepper. Top each fillet with lemon slices and 2 sprigs of thyme. Sprinkle each fillet with one-quarter of the zucchini and shallot mixture. Fold the parchment over.

4 Starting at the top, fold the edges of the parchment over, and continue all the way around to make a packet. Twist the end tightly to secure.

5 Arrange the 4 packets on a baking sheet. Bake for about 15 minutes. Place on plates; cut open. Serve immediately.

Per Serving Calories: 190; Total fat: 7g; Saturated fat: 1g; Cholesterol: 70mg; Sodium: 170mg; Potassium: 735mg; Total Carbohydrates: 5g; Fiber: 1g; Sugars: 2g; Protein: 27g; Magnesium: 40mg; Calcium: 25mg

Flounder with Tomatoes and Basil

SERVES 4 ▪ PREP TIME: 10 MINUTES ▪ COOK TIME: 20 MINUTES

- 1 pound cherry tomatoes
- 4 garlic cloves, sliced
- 2 tablespoons extra-virgin olive oil
- 2 tablespoons lemon juice
- 2 tablespoons basil, cut into ribbons
- ½ teaspoon kosher salt
- ¼ teaspoon freshly ground black pepper
- 4 (5- to 6-ounce) flounder fillets

Flounder, also known as fluke, is a flat fish with a light and delicate texture, mild flavor, and slightly sweet taste. It can be made in a variety of ways, but I like to bake it with a handful of ingredients for a simple, delicious meal.

1 Preheat the oven to 425°F.

2 In a baking dish, combine the tomatoes, garlic, olive oil, lemon juice, basil, salt, and black pepper; mix well. Bake for 5 minutes.

3 Remove the baking dish from the oven and arrange the flounder on top of the tomato mixture. Bake until the fish is opaque and begins to flake, about 10 to 15 minutes, depending on thickness.

SUBSTITUTION TIP: *Halibut or sole can be used in this dish in place of flounder.*

Per Serving Calories: 215; Total fat: 9g; Saturated fat: 1g; Cholesterol: 68mg; Sodium: 261mg; Potassium: 805mg; Total Carbohydrates: 6g; Fiber: 2g; Sugars: 3g; Protein: 28g; Magnesium: 60mg; Calcium: 45mg

Grilled Mahi-Mahi with Artichoke Caponata

SERVES 4 ▪ PREP TIME: 25 MINUTES ▪ COOK TIME: 30 MINUTES

2 tablespoons extra-virgin
 olive oil

2 celery stalks, diced

1 onion, diced

2 garlic cloves, minced

½ cup cherry
 tomatoes, chopped

¼ cup white wine

2 tablespoons white
 wine vinegar

1 (14-ounce) can artichoke
 hearts, drained
 and chopped

¼ cup green olives, pitted
 and chopped

1 tablespoon
 capers, chopped

¼ teaspoon red
 pepper flakes

2 tablespoons fresh
 basil, chopped

4 (5- to 6-ounces each)
 skinless mahi-mahi fillets

½ teaspoon kosher salt

¼ teaspoon freshly ground
 black pepper

Olive oil cooking spray

Caponata traditionally includes eggplant, raisins, and pine nuts among its list of ingredients. In this variation I replace those ingredients with artichoke hearts and green olives for a twist on the classic that stays true to the briny and bright nature of the dish. Most hearty fish would work in this recipe, including salmon, char, halibut, or tuna. I've paired it with grilled mahi-mahi, which is a firm tropical fish that holds up well to a variety of preparations.

1 Heat the olive oil in a large skillet or sauté pan over medium heat. Add the celery and onion, and sauté 4 to 5 minutes. Add the garlic and sauté 30 seconds. Add the tomatoes and cook 2 to 3 minutes. Add the wine and vinegar to deglaze the pan, increasing the heat to medium-high and scraping up any brown bits on the bottom of the pan.

2 Add the artichokes, olives, capers, and red pepper flakes and simmer, reducing the liquid by half, about 10 minutes. Mix in the basil.

3 Season the mahi-mahi with the salt and pepper. Heat a grill skillet or grill pan over medium-high heat and coat with olive oil cooking spray. Add the fish and cook 4 to 5 minutes per side. Serve topped with the artichoke caponata.

Per Serving Calories: 245; Total fat: 9g; Saturated fat: 1g; Cholesterol: 100mg; Sodium: 570mg; Potassium: 775mg; Total Carbohydrates: 10g; Fiber: 3g; Sugars: 3g; Protein: 28g; Magnesium: 55mg; Calcium: 50mg

Cod and Cauliflower Chowder

SERVES 4 ▪ PREP TIME: 15 MINUTES ▪ COOK TIME: 40 MINUTES

- 2 tablespoons extra-virgin olive oil
- 1 leek, white and light green parts only, cut in half lengthwise and sliced thinly
- 4 garlic cloves, sliced
- 1 medium head cauliflower, coarsely chopped
- 1 teaspoon kosher salt
- ¼ teaspoon freshly ground black pepper
- 2 pints cherry tomatoes
- 2 cups no-salt-added vegetable stock
- ¼ cup green olives, pitted and chopped
- 1 to 1½ pounds cod
- ¼ cup fresh parsley, minced

Classic fish chowder is typically full of heavy cream, flour-thickened broth, and potatoes. This version lightens things up and adds a boost of nutrients via cauliflower and cherry tomatoes. The olives add a little brininess, which helps to round out the dish. To cut down some prep time, you can use 2 cups of riced cauliflower instead of chopping the cauliflower. Serve this with some crusty whole-wheat bread or pita.

1 Heat the olive oil in a Dutch oven or large pot over medium heat. Add the leek and sauté until lightly golden brown, about 5 minutes. Add the garlic and sauté for 30 seconds. Add the cauliflower, salt, and black pepper and sauté 2 to 3 minutes.

2 Add the tomatoes and vegetable stock, increase the heat to high and bring to a boil, then turn the heat to low and simmer for 10 minutes.

3 Add the olives and mix together. Add the fish, cover, and simmer 20 minutes, or until fish is opaque and flakes easily. Gently mix in the parsley.

Per Serving Calories: 270; Total fat: 9g; Saturated fat: 1g; Cholesterol: 60mg; Sodium: 545mg; Potassium: 1475mg; Total Carbohydrates: 19g; Fiber: 5g; Sugars: 9g; Protein: 30g; Magnesium: 90mg; Calcium: 90mg

Sardine Bruschetta with Fennel and Lemon Crema

SERVES 4 ■ PREP TIME: 15 MINUTES

⅓ cup plain Greek yogurt

2 tablespoons mayonnaise

2 tablespoons lemon juice, divided

2 teaspoons lemon zest

¾ teaspoon kosher salt, divided

1 fennel bulb, cored and thinly sliced

¼ cup fresh parsley, chopped, plus more for garnish

¼ cup fresh mint, chopped, plus more for garnish

2 teaspoons extra-virgin olive oil

⅛ teaspoon freshly ground black pepper

8 slices multigrain bread, toasted

2 (4.4-ounce) cans smoked sardines

Sardines are tiny, inexpensive, and pack more omega-3 fatty acids per three-ounce serving than just about any other food. That's right, more than salmon and tuna! It is also one of a very few foods that is naturally high in vitamin D. Bountiful in the ocean, Pacific sardines are also an environmentally sustainable choice. This delicious bruschetta will win over everyone, even the sardine skeptics!

1 In a small bowl, combine the yogurt, mayonnaise, 1 tablespoon of the lemon juice, the lemon zest, and ¼ teaspoon of the salt.

2 In a separate small bowl, combine the remaining ½ teaspoon salt, the remaining 1 tablespoon lemon juice, the fennel, parsley, mint, olive oil, and black pepper.

3 Spoon 1 tablespoon of the yogurt mixture on each piece of toast. Divide the fennel mixture evenly on top of the yogurt mixture. Divide the sardines among the toasts, placing them on top of the fennel mixture. Garnish with more herbs, if desired.

SUBSTITUTION TIP: *Other smoked fish, including smoked trout or smoked salmon, would also work well in this dish.*

Per Serving Calories: 400; Total fat: 16g; Saturated fat: 2g; Cholesterol: 39mg; Sodium: 565mg; Potassium: 550mg; Total Carbohydrates: 51g; Fiber: 7g; Sugars: 6g; Protein: 16g; Magnesium: 95mg; Calcium: 170mg

Chopped Tuna Salad

SERVES 4 ▪ PREP TIME: 15 MINUTES

2 tablespoons extra-virgin olive oil

2 tablespoons lemon juice

2 teaspoons Dijon mustard

½ teaspoon kosher salt

¼ teaspoon freshly ground black pepper

12 olives, pitted and chopped

½ cup celery, diced

½ cup red onion, diced

½ cup red bell pepper, diced

½ cup fresh parsley, chopped

2 (6-ounce) cans no-salt-added tuna packed in water, drained

6 cups baby spinach

Canned tuna is a constant in my pantry, but it can get ho-hum if it's always paired with mayo or plain yogurt. This chopped tuna salad features Mediterranean vegetables and herbs for a refreshing twist that is anything but boring. This tuna salad wins every time, combining flavor and crunch with vital nutrients like omega-3 fatty acids, iron, and vitamin C. Don't feel like baby spinach? Sub in any greens as the base for this dish.

1 In a medium bowl, whisk together the olive oil, lemon juice, mustard, salt, and black pepper. Add in the olives, celery, onion, bell pepper, and parsley and mix well. Add the tuna and gently incorporate.

2 Divide the spinach evenly among 4 plates or bowls. Spoon the tuna salad evenly on top of the spinach.

SUBSTITUTION TIP: *Canned salmon can be used in place of canned tuna in this dish. Look for skinless, boneless salmon for the best results.*

Per Serving Calories: 220; Total fat: 11g; Saturated fat: 1g; Cholesterol: 38mg; Sodium: 396mg; Potassium: 420mg; Total Carbohydrates: 7g; Fiber: 2g; Sugars: 2g; Protein: 25g; Magnesium: 45mg; Calcium: 70mg

Monkfish with Sautéed Leeks, Fennel, and Tomatoes

SERVES 4 ■ PREP TIME: 20 MINUTES ■ COOK TIME: 35 MINUTES

- 1 to 1½ pounds monkfish
- 3 tablespoons lemon juice, divided
- 1 teaspoon kosher salt, divided
- ⅛ teaspoon freshly ground black pepper
- 2 tablespoons extra-virgin olive oil
- 1 leek, white and light green parts only, sliced in half lengthwise and thinly sliced
- ½ onion, julienned
- 3 garlic cloves, minced
- 2 bulbs fennel, cored and thinly sliced, plus ¼ cup fronds for garnish
- 1 (14.5-ounce) can no-salt-added diced tomatoes
- 2 tablespoons fresh parsley, chopped
- 2 tablespoons fresh oregano, chopped
- ¼ teaspoon red pepper flakes

Monkfish has a tight, meaty texture that is often compared to lobster meat and referred to as "poor man's lobster." The flesh is lean, light gray to white, tastes mild, and is easily prepared in a variety of ways. We typically eat the tail meat, so look for skinless tail fillets at your local grocery store or fishmonger.

1 Place the fish in a medium baking dish and add 2 tablespoons of the lemon juice, ¼ teaspoon of the salt, and the black pepper. Place in the refrigerator.

2 Heat the olive oil in a large skillet or sauté pan over medium heat. Add the leek and onion and sauté until translucent, about 3 minutes. Add the garlic and sauté for 30 seconds. Add the fennel and sauté 4 to 5 minutes. Add the tomatoes and simmer for 2 to 3 minutes.

3 Stir in the parsley, oregano, red pepper flakes, the remaining ¾ teaspoon salt, and the remaining 1 tablespoon lemon juice. Place the fish on top of the leek mixture, cover, and simmer for 20 to 25 minutes, turning over halfway through, until the fish is opaque and pulls apart easily. Garnish with the fennel fronds.

SUBSTITUTION TIP: *Switch the monkfish for sea bass, snapper, mahi-mahi, or halibut.*

Per Serving Calories: 220; Total fat: 9g; Saturated fat: 2g; Cholesterol: 35mg; Sodium: 345mg; Potassium: 800mg; Total Carbohydrates: 11g; Fiber: 3g; Sugars: 6g; Protein: 22g; Magnesium: 45mg; Calcium: 70mg

Caramelized Fennel and Sardines with Penne

SERVES 4 ▪ PREP TIME: 15 MINUTES ▪ COOK TIME: 30 MINUTES

8 ounces whole-wheat
  penne

2 tablespoons extra-virgin
  olive oil

1 bulb fennel, cored
  and thinly sliced, plus
  ¼ cup fronds

2 celery stalks, thinly sliced,
  plus ½ cup leaves

4 garlic cloves, sliced

¾ teaspoon kosher salt

¼ teaspoon freshly ground
  black pepper

Zest of 1 lemon

Juice of 1 lemon

2 (4.4-ounce) cans
  boneless/skinless
  sardines packed in olive
  oil, undrained

This is my version of the classic Sicilian dish *pasta con le sarde*, or pasta with sardines. The sweet, caramel flavor of the fennel and celery combines well with the brightness of the lemon zest and the richness of the sardines. For extra acidity, squeeze in some lemon juice as well. Any pasta will work with this dish, so grab what you've got in your pantry and get going!

1 Cook the penne according to the package directions. Drain, reserving 1 cup pasta water.

2 Heat the olive oil in a large skillet or sauté pan over medium heat. Add the fennel and celery and cook, stirring often, until tender and golden, about 10 to 12 minutes. Add the garlic and cook for 1 minute.

3 Add the penne, reserved pasta water, salt, and black pepper. Increase the heat to medium-high and cook for 1 to 2 minutes.

4 Remove the pan from the heat and stir in the lemon zest, lemon juice, fennel fronds, and celery leaves. Break the sardines into bite-size pieces and gently mix in, along with the oil they were packed in.

Per Serving Calories: 400; Total fat: 15g; Saturated fat: 2g; Cholesterol: 81mg; Sodium: 530mg; Potassium: 610mg; Total Carbohydrates: 46g; Fiber: 6g; Sugars: 4g; Protein: 22g; Magnesium: 30mg; Calcium: 265mg

Cioppino

SERVES 4 ▪ PREP TIME: 15 MINUTES ▪ COOK TIME: 35 MINUTES

2 tablespoons extra-virgin
olive oil

1 onion, diced

1 bulb fennel, diced, plus
½ cup fronds for garnish

1 quart no-salt-added
vegetable stock

4 garlic cloves, smashed

8 thyme sprigs

1 teaspoon kosher salt

¼ teaspoon red
pepper flakes

1 dried bay leaf

1 bunch kale, stemmed
and chopped

1 dozen littleneck clams
tightly closed, scrubbed

1 pound fish (cod, halibut,
and bass are all
good choices)

¼ cup fresh
parsley, chopped

Cioppino is often referred to as a "fisherman's stew."
It uses whatever the fresh catch of the day may be—fish
and shellfish. There are countless variations, so add
whatever seafood you like! In this version we use clams
and white fish, but mussels, crab, and shrimp are also
great options. Onion, fennel, garlic, and kale give the dish
a boost of nutrients, including vitamin K and fiber. Serve
with freshly baked whole-wheat bread for dipping.

1 Heat the olive oil in a large stock pot over medium heat.
Add the onion and fennel and sauté about 5 minutes. Add
the vegetable stock, garlic, thyme, salt, red pepper flakes,
and bay leaf. Increase the heat to medium-high, and bring
to a simmer. Add the kale, cover, and simmer 5 minutes.

2 Carefully add the clams, cover, and simmer about
15 minutes until they open. Remove the clams and set
aside. Discard any clams that do not open.

3 Add the fish, cover, and simmer 5 to 10 minutes,
depending on the thickness of the fish, until opaque and
easily separated. Gently mix in the parsley.

4 Divide the cioppino among 4 bowls. Place 3 clams in
each bowl and garnish with the fennel fronds.

Per Serving Calories: 285; Total fat: 9g; Saturated fat: 1g;
Cholesterol: 73mg; Sodium: 570mg; Potassium: 1220mg;
Total Carbohydrates: 19g; Fiber: 3g; Sugars: 7g; Protein: 32g;
Magnesium: 100mg; Calcium: 195mg

Green Goddess Crab Salad with Endive

SERVES 4 ▪ PREP TIME: 10 MINUTES ▪ COOK TIME: 10 MINUTES

1 pound lump crabmeat

⅔ cup plain Greek yogurt

3 tablespoons mayonnaise

3 tablespoons fresh chives, chopped, plus additional for garnish

3 tablespoons fresh parsley, chopped, plus additional for garnish

3 tablespoons fresh basil, chopped, plus additional for garnish

Zest of 1 lemon

Juice of 1 lemon

½ teaspoon kosher salt

¼ teaspoon freshly ground black pepper

4 endives, ends cut off and leaves separated

I love a good shellfish-based salad. This one features succulent crabmeat as the base. You can easily find canned or packaged crabmeat in the seafood area of many grocery stores, but feel free to swap out the crab for shrimp or lobster. For creamy dressings, plain Greek yogurt is my secret weapon. Greek yogurt delivers extra protein and a lovely tang without the saturated fat often found in a mayo-based dressing. This dish has a ton of herbs and a dash of citrus for balance. Some people find endive to be bitter, so feel free to swap it out for crunchy romaine or tender butter lettuce if you prefer.

1 In a medium bowl, combine the crab, yogurt, mayonnaise, chives, parsley, basil, lemon zest, lemon juice, salt, and black pepper and mix until well combined.

2 Place the endive leaves on 4 salad plates. Divide the crab mixture evenly on top of the endive. Garnish with additional herbs, if desired.

Per Serving Calories: 200; Total fat: 9g; Saturated fat: 2g; Cholesterol: 119mg; Sodium: 570mg; Potassium: 540mg; Total Carbohydrates: 44g; Fiber: 2g; Sugars: 2g; Protein: 25g; Magnesium: 55mg; Calcium: 180mg

Seared Scallops with Blood Orange Glaze

SERVES 4 ■ PREP TIME: 10 MINUTES ■ COOK TIME: 20 MINUTES

3 tablespoons extra-virgin olive oil, divided

3 garlic cloves, minced

½ teaspoon kosher salt, divided

4 blood oranges, juiced

1 teaspoon blood orange zest

½ teaspoon red pepper flakes

1 pound scallops, small side muscle removed

¼ teaspoon freshly ground black pepper

¼ cup fresh chives, chopped

Cooking scallops is an easy, healthy go-to meal. Minimal prep, less than five minutes to cook, and they're ready to go! When buying scallops, look for "dry" scallops, which taste better and have not been treated with any chemical additives. Be sure to pat the outside of the scallops dry with a paper towel prior to seasoning and cooking. Keep enough room between the scallops in your pan to ensure they sear nicely and don't steam each other. You should hear a sizzling noise when you place them in the pan. The sweet and spicy citrus glaze pairs perfectly with seared scallops. For a spicier sauce, add the red pepper flakes at the beginning of step 1 with the orange juice and zest.

1 Heat 1 tablespoon of the olive oil in a small saucepan over medium-high heat. Add the garlic and ¼ teaspoon of the salt and sauté for 30 seconds. Add the orange juice and zest, bring to a boil, reduce the heat to medium-low, and cook for about 20 minutes, or until the liquid reduces by half and becomes a thicker syrup consistency. Take off the heat and mix in the red pepper flakes.

2 Pat the scallops dry with a paper towel and season with the remaining ¼ teaspoon salt and the black pepper. Heat the remaining 2 tablespoons of olive oil in a large skillet on medium-high heat. Add the scallops gently and sear. Cook on each side about 2 minutes. If cooking in 2 batches, use 1 tablespoon of oil per batch.

3 Serve the scallops with the blood orange glaze and garnish with the chives.

Per Serving Calories: 140; Total fat: 4g; Saturated fat: 1g; Cholesterol: 27mg; Sodium: 570mg; Potassium: 380mg; Total Carbohydrates: 12g; Fiber: 0g; Sugars: 5g; Protein: 15g; Magnesium: 35mg; Calcium: 25mg

Lemon Garlic Shrimp

SERVES 4 ▪ PREP TIME: 15 MINUTES ▪ COOK TIME: 10 MINUTES

2 tablespoons extra-virgin
    olive oil

3 garlic cloves, sliced

½ teaspoon kosher salt

¼ teaspoon red
    pepper flakes

1 pound large shrimp,
    peeled and deveined

½ cup white wine

3 tablespoons fresh
    parsley, minced

Zest of ½ lemon

Juice of ½ lemon

The size of a shrimp is determined by the number of individual shrimp it takes to make up a pound. For example, a label of 16/20 means that there are between 16 and 20 shrimp in a pound. Basically, the smaller the number, the bigger the shrimp. For this dish, I recommend 31/36 (large) or 26/30 (extra-large) shrimp. Purchasing uncooked cleaned shrimp that are already peeled and deveined will save a lot of prep time. For extra protein and fiber, serve this spicy lemon shrimp over quinoa, which will also help to soak up the tasty sauce. Looking to add extra vegetables? Try it with zucchini noodles.

1 Heat the olive oil in a wok or large skillet over medium-high heat. Add the garlic, salt, and red pepper flakes and sauté until the garlic starts to brown, 30 seconds to 1 minute.

2 Add the shrimp and cook until pink, 2 to 3 minutes on each side. Pour in the wine and deglaze the wok, scraping up any flavorful brown bits, for 1 to 2 minutes.

3 Turn off the heat; mix in the parsley, lemon zest, and lemon juice.

INGREDIENT TIP: *Sautéing the garlic and red pepper flakes in the oil before adding the shrimp allows the aromatics to infuse the oil, providing more flavor overall. But be warned: This makes the dish spicier! If you are not a fan of spicy food or just want more control over the level of spiciness, add the red pepper flakes at the end when you stir in the lemon and parsley.*

Per Serving Calories: 200; Total fat: 9g; Saturated fat: 1g; Cholesterol: 170mg; Sodium: 310mg; Potassium: 250mg; Total Carbohydrates: 3g; Fiber: 0g; Sugars: 0g; Protein: 23g; Magnesium: 45mg; Calcium: 70mg

Shrimp Fra Diavolo

SERVES 4 ▪ PREP TIME: 10 MINUTES ▪ COOK TIME: 10 MINUTES

2 tablespoons extra-virgin olive oil

1 onion, diced small

1 fennel bulb, cored and diced small, plus ¼ cup fronds for garnish

1 bell pepper, diced small

½ teaspoon dried oregano

½ teaspoon dried thyme

½ teaspoon kosher salt

¼ teaspoon red pepper flakes

1 (14.5-ounce) can no-salt-added diced tomatoes

1 pound shrimp, peeled and deveined

Juice of 1 lemon

Zest of 1 lemon

2 tablespoons fresh parsley, chopped, for garnish

"Fra diavolo" means "Brother Devil" in Italian and typically refers to a spicy, tomato-based sauce. My Shrimp Fra Diavolo is a delicious way to add a flavor kick to dinner, along with good-for-you omega-3 fatty acids. Serve the shrimp over brown rice or angel hair pasta (get it?) and alongside Roasted Broccoli with Tahini Yogurt Sauce (page 44) for a delicious, well-balanced meal.

1 Heat the olive oil in a large skillet or sauté pan over medium heat. Add the onion, fennel, bell pepper, oregano, thyme, salt, and red pepper flakes and sauté until translucent, about 5 minutes.

2 Deglaze the pan with the juice from the canned tomatoes, scraping up any brown bits, and bring to a boil. Add the diced tomatoes and the shrimp. Lower heat to a simmer, cover, and cook until the shrimp are cooked through, about 3 minutes.

3 Turn off the heat. Add the lemon juice and lemon zest, and toss well to combine. Garnish with the parsley and the fennel fronds.

Per Serving Calories: 240; Total fat: 9g; Saturated fat: 1g; Cholesterol: 170mg; Sodium: 335mg; Potassium: 445mg; Total Carbohydrates: 13g; Fiber: 3g; Sugars: 7g; Protein: 25g; Magnesium: 55mg; Calcium: 105mg

Shrimp with White Beans and Feta

SERVES 4 ▪ PREP TIME: 15 MINUTES ▪ COOK TIME: 15 MINUTES

3 tablespoons lemon juice, divided

2 tablespoons extra-virgin olive oil, divided

½ teaspoon kosher salt, divided

1 pound shrimp, peeled and deveined

1 large shallot, diced

¼ cup no-salt-added vegetable stock

1 (15-ounce) can no-salt-added or low-sodium cannellini beans, rinsed and drained

¼ cup fresh mint, chopped

1 teaspoon lemon zest

1 tablespoon white wine vinegar

¼ teaspoon freshly ground black pepper

¼ cup crumbled feta cheese, for garnish

This riff on Tuscan-style beans gets robust seafood flavor from simmering the beans together with the shrimp. To keep the shrimp plump and juicy, we marinate them briefly before adding them to the pan and cook them gently. Canned beans and other pantry staples make this dish fast and perfect for any time of year.

1 In a small bowl, whisk together 1 tablespoon of the lemon juice, 1 tablespoon of the olive oil, and ¼ teaspoon of the salt. Add the shrimp and set aside.

2 Heat the remaining 1 tablespoon olive oil in a large skillet or sauté pan over medium heat. Add the shallot and sauté until translucent, about 2 to 3 minutes. Add the vegetable stock and deglaze the pan, scraping up any brown bits, and bring to a boil. Add the beans and shrimp. Reduce the heat to low, cover, and simmer until the shrimp are cooked through, about 3 to 4 minutes.

3 Turn off the heat and add the mint, lemon zest, vinegar, and black pepper. Stir gently to combine. Garnish with the feta.

Per Serving Calories: 340; Total fat: 11g; Saturated fat: 3g; Cholesterol: 181mg; Sodium: 415mg; Potassium: 770mg; Total Carbohydrates: 28g; Fiber: 6g; Sugars: 3g; Protein: 32g; Magnesium: 100mg; Calcium: 195mg

Lemon Chicken
with Artichokes and
Crispy Kale, page 130

Poultry and Meat

Crispy Mediterranean Chicken Thighs

SERVES 6 ▪ PREP TIME: 5 MINUTES ▪ COOK TIME: 30 TO 35 MINUTES

2 tablespoons extra-virgin
olive oil

2 teaspoons dried rosemary

1½ teaspoons
ground cumin

1½ teaspoons
ground coriander

¾ teaspoon dried oregano

⅛ teaspoon salt

6 bone-in, skin-on chicken
thighs (about 3 pounds)

Amazingly simple and delicious, roasted chicken thighs are easy to prepare with only a few ingredients and a single pan. No need to turn or move them while cooking; the chicken will sear and crisp right in the oven. Be sure to use a rimmed baking sheet to catch (and keep) the natural juices right in the pan. This is the ideal quick weeknight dinner, especially when served alongside Roasted Harissa Carrots (page 47).

1 Preheat the oven to 450°F. Line a baking sheet with parchment paper.

2 Place the olive oil and spices into a large bowl and mix together, making a paste. Add the chicken and mix together until evenly coated. Place on the prepared baking sheet.

3 Bake for 30 to 35 minutes, or until golden brown and the chicken registers an internal temperature of 165°F.

INGREDIENT TIP: *To decrease overall saturated fat in the dish, remove the chicken skin prior to mixing with the spices. The finished chicken will still be flavorful, but without a crispy skin.*

VARIATION TIP: *To add a bit of brightness to the dish, serve with lemon wedges or squeeze half a lemon over the chicken thighs before serving.*

Per Serving Calories: 440; Total fat: 34g; Saturated fat: 9g; Cholesterol: 172mg; Sodium: 180mg; Potassium: 395mg; Total Carbohydrates: 1g; Fiber: 0g; Sugars: 0g; Protein: 30g; Magnesium: 40mg; Calcium: 30mg

Greek Turkey Burger

SERVES 4 ▪ PREP TIME: 10 MINUTES ▪ COOK TIME: 10 MINUTES

1 pound ground turkey

1 medium zucchini, grated

¼ cup whole-wheat
    bread crumbs

¼ cup red onion, minced

¼ cup crumbled
    feta cheese

1 large egg, beaten

1 garlic clove, minced

1 tablespoon fresh
    oregano, chopped

1 teaspoon kosher salt

¼ teaspoon freshly ground
    black pepper

1 tablespoon extra-virgin
    olive oil

Adding herbs, vegetables, and cheese to a burger recipe provides moisture, texture, and flavor (not to mention an extra dose of nutrients), allowing us to cut back on the amount of ground meat or poultry—and saturated fat—in the burger without sacrificing taste. This recipe incorporates some ingredients typically found in a Greek salad, such as red onion, oregano, and feta cheese. Serve on a bed of greens with Cherry Tomato Bruschetta (page 49) and Cucumbers with Feta, Mint, and Sumac (page 48).

1 In a large bowl, combine the turkey, zucchini, bread crumbs, onion, feta cheese, egg, garlic, oregano, salt, and black pepper, and mix well. Shape into 4 equal patties.

2 Heat the olive oil in a large nonstick grill pan or skillet over medium-high heat. Add the burgers to the pan and reduce the heat to medium. Cook on one side for 5 minutes, then flip and cook the other side for 5 minutes more.

SUBSTITUTION TIP: *Any summer squash can be used in this recipe, so feel free to swap out the zucchini for yellow squash or pattypan squash.*

Per Serving Calories: 285; Total fat: 16g; Saturated fat: 5g; Cholesterol: 139mg; Sodium: 465mg; Potassium: 415mg; Total Carbohydrates: 9g; Fiber: 2g; Sugars: 2g; Protein: 26g; Magnesium: 40mg; Calcium: 90mg

Harissa Yogurt Chicken Thighs

SERVES 4 ▪ PREP TIME: 5 MINUTES, PLUS 15 MINUTES TO MARINATE
COOK TIME: 25 MINUTES

½ cup plain Greek yogurt

2 tablespoons harissa

1 tablespoon lemon juice

½ teaspoon kosher salt

¼ teaspoon freshly ground
    black pepper

1½ pounds boneless,
    skinless chicken thighs

This simple recipe uses only a handful of ingredients, all of which you may already have on hand. It is a tasty, quick, and healthy dish that you are sure to have on repeat. The spice level varies from mild to hot based on the harissa you use. To get a full dinner on the table, add a few diced potatoes and some broccoli florets to the baking sheet and roast along with the chicken. If you're like me and love a good dipping sauce, the chicken goes perfectly with Tzatziki (page 151).

1 In a bowl, combine the yogurt, harissa, lemon juice, salt, and black pepper. Add the chicken and mix together. Marinate for at least 15 minutes, and up to 4 hours in the refrigerator.

2 Preheat the oven to 425°F. Line a baking sheet with parchment paper or foil. Remove the chicken thighs from the marinade and arrange in a single layer on the baking sheet. Roast for 20 minutes, turning the chicken over halfway.

3 Change the oven temperature to broil. Broil the chicken until golden brown in spots, 2 to 3 minutes.

Per Serving Calories: 190; Total fat: 10g; Saturated fat: 2g; Cholesterol: 107mg; Sodium: 230mg; Potassium: 300mg; Total Carbohydrates: 1g; Fiber: 0g; Sugars: 1g; Protein: 24g; Magnesium: 28mg; Calcium: 24mg

Sumac Chicken with Cauliflower and Carrots

SERVES 4 ▪ PREP TIME: 15 MINUTES ▪ COOK TIME: 40 MINUTES

3 tablespoons extra-virgin olive oil

1 tablespoon ground sumac

1 teaspoon kosher salt

½ teaspoon ground cumin

¼ teaspoon freshly ground black pepper

1½ pounds bone-in chicken thighs and drumsticks

1 medium cauliflower, cut into 1-inch florets

2 carrots, peeled and cut into 1-inch rounds

1 lemon, cut into ¼-inch-thick slices

1 tablespoon lemon juice

¼ cup fresh parsley, chopped

¼ cup fresh mint, chopped

Full of lemon and spice, this easy sumac chicken sheet pan meal is healthy and fast. Adding a baked potato, whole grain, or legume side dish, such as French Lentil Salad with Parsley and Mint (page 74), creates the perfect weeknight dinner solution. The skin stays on in this recipe, but you can remove it to decrease the overall saturated fat in the dish. The chicken will still be flavorful and moist.

1 Preheat the oven to 425°F. Line a baking sheet with parchment paper or foil.

2 In a large bowl, whisk together the olive oil, sumac, salt, cumin, and black pepper. Add the chicken, cauliflower, and carrots and toss until thoroughly coated with the oil and spice mixture.

3 Arrange the cauliflower, carrots, and chicken in a single layer on the baking sheet. Top with the lemon slices. Roast for 40 minutes, tossing the vegetables once halfway through. Sprinkle the lemon juice over the chicken and vegetables and garnish with the parsley and mint.

Per Serving Calories: 510; Total fat: 38g; Saturated fat: 9g; Cholesterol: 158mg; Sodium: 490mg; Potassium: 930mg; Total Carbohydrates: 13g; Fiber: 4g; Sugars: 5g; Protein: 31g; Magnesium: 63mg; Calcium: 73mg

Lemon Chicken with Artichokes and Crispy Kale

SERVES 4 ▪ PREP TIME: 15 MINUTES, PLUS 30 MINUTES TO MARINATE
COOK TIME: 35 MINUTES

3 tablespoons extra-virgin olive oil, divided

2 tablespoons lemon juice

Zest of 1 lemon

2 garlic cloves, minced

2 teaspoons dried rosemary

½ teaspoon kosher salt

¼ teaspoon freshly ground black pepper

1½ pounds boneless, skinless chicken breast

2 (14-ounce) cans artichoke hearts, drained

1 bunch (about 6 ounces) lacinato kale, stemmed and torn or chopped into pieces

This sheet pan dinner is a great way to get a meal on the table quickly and without a lot of cleanup. I like to serve this dish with roasted sweet potatoes. Simply dice up some sweet potatoes, toss them with olive oil, salt, and pepper, put them on a second sheet pan, and bake them simultaneously with the chicken.

1 In a large bowl or zip-top bag, combine 2 tablespoons of the olive oil, the lemon juice, lemon zest, garlic, rosemary, salt, and black pepper. Mix well and then add the chicken and artichokes. Marinate for at least 30 minutes, and up to 4 hours in the refrigerator.

2 Preheat the oven to 350°F. Line a baking sheet with parchment paper or foil. Remove the chicken and artichokes from the marinade and spread them in a single layer on the baking sheet. Roast for 15 minutes, turn the chicken over, and roast another 15 minutes. Remove the baking sheet and put the chicken, artichokes, and juices on a platter or large plate. Tent with foil to keep warm.

3 Change the oven temperature to broil. In a large bowl, combine the kale with the remaining 1 tablespoon of the olive oil. Arrange the kale on the baking sheet and broil until golden brown in spots and as crispy as you like, about 3 to 5 minutes. Place the kale on top of the chicken and artichokes.

INGREDIENT TIP: *I like to use lacinato kale, which is a flatter variety. The smoother leaves absorb more heat from the broiler, cook more evenly, and become crispier versus curly varieties of kale, which have crevices and do not cook as effectively under the broiler.*

Per Serving Calories: 430; Total fat: 16g; Saturated fat: 3g; Cholesterol: 124mg; Sodium: 350mg; Potassium: 1,365mg; Total Carbohydrates: 29g; Fiber: 19g; Sugars: 3g; Protein: 46g; Magnesium: 155mg; Calcium: 125mg

Za'atar Chicken Tenders

SERVES 4 ▪ PREP TIME: 5 MINUTES ▪ COOK TIME: 15 MINUTES

Olive oil cooking spray

1 pound chicken tenders

1½ tablespoons za'atar

½ teaspoon kosher salt

¼ teaspoon freshly ground
    black pepper

Put a sophisticated spin on classic chicken fingers. This perfectly tender chicken covered in a crispy za'atar crust is done in less than 30 minutes with only a small list of ingredients. Try some zesty dressings on the side, like Lemon Tahini Dressing (page 153) or Salsa Verde (page 152). Add some roasted potato wedges and crisp cucumber spears to complete the meal.

1 Preheat the oven to 450°F. Line a baking sheet with parchment paper or foil and lightly spray with olive oil cooking spray.

2 In a large bowl, combine the chicken, za'atar, salt, and black pepper. Mix together well, covering the chicken tenders fully. Arrange in a single layer on the baking sheet and bake for 15 minutes, turning the chicken over once halfway through the cooking time.

Per Serving Calories: 145; Total fat: 4g; Saturated fat: 1g; Cholesterol: 83mg; Sodium: 190mg; Potassium: 390mg; Total Carbohydrates: 0g; Fiber: 0g; Sugars: 0g; Protein: 26g; Magnesium: 37mg; Calcium: 13mg

Chicken Stew with Artichokes, Capers, and Olives

SERVES 4 ✳ PREP TIME: 20 MINUTES ✳ COOK TIME: 35 MINUTES

1½ pounds boneless, skinless chicken thighs

1 teaspoon kosher salt, divided

¼ teaspoon freshly ground black pepper

2 tablespoons olive oil

1 onion, julienned

4 garlic cloves, sliced

1 teaspoon ground turmeric

1 teaspoon ground cumin

½ teaspoon ground coriander

½ teaspoon ground cinnamon

¼ teaspoon red pepper flakes

1 dried bay leaf

1¼ cups no-salt-added chicken stock

¼ cup white wine vinegar

2 tablespoons lemon juice

1 tablespoon lemon zest

1 (14-ounce) can artichoke hearts, drained

¼ cup olives, pitted and chopped

1 teaspoon capers, rinsed and chopped

1 tablespoon fresh mint, chopped

1 tablespoon fresh parsley, chopped

This hearty stew is seasoned with a blend of flavorful and healthy spices and herbs, including turmeric, cumin, and mint. Feel free to use thawed, frozen artichoke hearts instead of the can; serve over brown rice and you've got a full meal.

1 Season the chicken with ½ teaspoon of salt and pepper.

2 Heat the olive oil in a large skillet or sauté pan over medium heat. Add the chicken and sauté 2 to 3 minutes per side. Transfer to a plate and set aside.

3 Add the onion to the same pan and sauté until translucent, about 5 minutes. Add the garlic and sauté 30 seconds. Add the remaining ½ teaspoon salt, the turmeric, cumin, coriander, cinnamon, red pepper flakes, and bay leaf and sauté 30 seconds.

4 Add ¼ cup of the chicken stock and increase the heat to medium-high to deglaze the pan, scraping up any brown bits on the bottom. Add the remaining 1 cup stock, the lemon juice, and lemon zest. Cover, lower the heat to low, and simmer for 10 minutes.

5 Add the artichokes, olives, and capers and mix well. Add the reserved chicken and nestle it into the mixture. Simmer, uncovered, until the chicken fully cooks through, about 10 to 15 minutes. Garnish with the mint and parsley.

Per Serving Calories: 500; Total fat: 36g; Saturated fat: 9g; Cholesterol: 167mg; Sodium: 570mg; Potassium: 480mg; Total Carbohydrates: 11g; Fiber: 3g; Sugars: 3g; Protein: 30g; Magnesium: 40mg; Calcium: 40mg

Braised Chicken with Roasted Bell Peppers

SERVES 8 ▪ PREP TIME: 30 MINUTES ▪ COOK TIME: 1 HOUR, 15 MINUTES

2 tablespoons extra-virgin olive oil

4 pounds bone-in chicken, breast and thighs, skin removed

1½ teaspoon kosher salt, divided

¼ teaspoon freshly ground black pepper

1 onion, julienned

6 garlic cloves, sliced

1 cup white wine

2 pounds tomatoes, chopped

¼ teaspoon red pepper flakes

3 bell peppers (any colors you like) or 2 jars roasted red peppers, drained

⅓ cup fresh parsley, chopped

1 tablespoon lemon juice

I love everything about a rich, hearty braised chicken dish, from the flavorful broth to the moist braised chicken to the slightly sweet roasted peppers—it just works. This one-pot meal is terrific for entertaining friends or family, or simply to ensure there are leftovers to be frozen and enjoyed again at a later date. I like to use bone-in chicken breast and thighs, but you can use bone-in or boneless thighs, breasts, wings, or drumsticks. It should all work well and taste wonderful.

1 Heat the olive oil in a large Dutch oven or pot over medium-high heat. Season the chicken with ¾ teaspoon of the salt and the pepper. Add half the chicken to the pot and brown about 2 minutes on each side. Transfer to a plate, and repeat with the remaining half of the chicken.

2 Lower the heat to medium and add the onion. Sauté for about 5 minutes. Add the garlic and sauté for 30 seconds. Add the wine, increase the heat to medium-high, and bring to a boil to deglaze the pot, scraping up any brown bits on the bottom. Reduce the liquid by half, about 5 to 7 minutes. Add the tomatoes, red pepper flakes, and the remaining ¾ teaspoon salt and mix well. Add the chicken back to the pot, cover, reduce the heat to low, and simmer for 40 minutes, turning the chicken halfway through the cooking time.

3 While the chicken cooks, prepare the roasted bell peppers. If you are using raw peppers, please refer to the roasting method on page 53. If using jarred roasted red peppers, move on to step 4.

4 Chop the bell peppers into 1-inch pieces and set aside.

5 Once the chicken is cooked through, transfer it to a plate.

6 Increase the heat to high and bring the mixture to a boil. Reduce by half, about 10 minutes.

7 When the chicken is cool enough to handle, remove the meat from the bone and return it to the pot with the bell peppers. Simmer 5 minutes to heat through. Stir in the parsley and lemon juice.

Per Serving Calories: 490; Total fat: 28g; Saturated fat: 7g; Cholesterol: 198mg; Sodium: 480mg; Potassium: 980mg; Total Carbohydrates: 11g; Fiber: 3g; Sugars: 6g; Protein: 43g; Magnesium: 70mg; Calcium: 45mg

Yogurt-Marinated Chicken Kebabs

SERVES 4 ▪ PREP TIME: 10 MINUTES ▪ COOK TIME: 20 MINUTES

½ cup plain Greek yogurt

1 tablespoon lemon juice

½ teaspoon ground cumin

½ teaspoon
ground coriander

½ teaspoon kosher salt

¼ teaspoon cayenne pepper

1½ pound skinless,
boneless chicken breast,
cut into 1-inch cubes

Yogurt makes a great marinade base for meat and poultry. The acids in the yogurt tenderize the chicken and help it absorb the spices and lemon juice. These kebabs can be cooked in the oven or outside on the grill. If using bamboo skewers, soak them in water for at least 30 minutes prior to placing chicken on them. Serve these kebabs with Yogurt Tahini Dressing (page 154) for dipping.

1 In a large bowl or zip-top bag, combine the yogurt, lemon juice, cumin, coriander, salt, and cayenne pepper. Mix together thoroughly and then add the chicken. Marinate for at least 30 minutes, and up to overnight in the refrigerator.

2 Preheat the oven to 425°F. Line a baking sheet with parchment paper or foil. Remove the chicken from the marinade and thread it on 4 bamboo or metal skewers.

3 Bake for 20 minutes, turning the chicken over once halfway through the cooking time.

Per Serving Calories: 170; Total fat: 4g; Saturated fat: 1g; Cholesterol: 92mg; Sodium: 390mg; Potassium: 515mg; Total Carbohydrates: 1g; Fiber: 0g; Sugars: 1g; Protein: 31g; Magnesium: 40mg; Calcium: 35mg

Beef Kofta

SERVES 4 ▪ PREP TIME: 10 MINUTES ▪ COOK TIME: 20 MINUTES

Olive oil cooking spray

½ onion, roughly chopped

1-inch piece ginger, peeled

2 garlic cloves, peeled

⅓ cup fresh parsley

⅓ cup fresh mint

1 pound ground beef

1 tablespoon ground cumin

1 tablespoon
    ground coriander

1 teaspoon
    ground cinnamon

¾ teaspoon kosher salt

½ teaspoon ground sumac

¼ teaspoon ground cloves

¼ teaspoon freshly ground
    black pepper

There are many types of kofta, which is sometimes spelled kefta, kafta, or kufta. It is a Persian word meaning "ground or pounded." Kofta can be meat, poultry, or seafood, and is blended with an assortment of onion, garlic, herbs, and spices. In this recipe, beef is shaped into meatballs with a variety of warming spices. It goes well with Tzatziki (page 151) and Wild Rice Salad with Chickpeas and Pickled Radish (page 70).

1 Preheat the oven to 400°F. Grease a 12-cup muffin tin with olive oil cooking spray.

2 In a food processor, add the onion, ginger, garlic, parsley, and mint; process until minced.

3 Place the onion mixture in a large bowl. Add the beef, cumin, coriander, cinnamon, salt, sumac, cloves, and black pepper and mix together thoroughly with your hands.

4 Divide the beef mixture into 12 balls and place each one in a cup of the prepared muffin tin. Bake for 20 minutes.

SUBSTITUTION TIP: *Ground lamb, turkey, chicken, and pork should all work well here. If using meat with less fat, such as poultry breast or pork, the cooking time may decrease by 2 to 3 minutes so that the kofta does not dry out.*

Per Serving Calories: 225; Total fat: 12g; Saturated fat: 5g; Cholesterol: 74mg; Sodium: 290mg; Potassium: 495mg; Total Carbohydrates: 5g; Fiber: 2g; Sugars: 1g; Protein: 24g; Magnesium: 40mg; Calcium: 65mg

Mediterranean Chimichurri Skirt Steak

SERVES 4 ▪ PREP TIME: 10 MINUTES, PLUS 30 MINUTES TO MARINATE
COOK TIME: 15 MINUTES

¾ cup fresh mint

¾ cup fresh parsley

⅔ cup extra-virgin olive oil

⅓ cup lemon juice

Zest of 1 lemon

2 tablespoons dried oregano

4 garlic cloves, peeled

½ teaspoon red
 pepper flakes

½ teaspoon kosher salt

1 to 1½ pounds skirt steak,
 cut in half if longer than
 grill pan

Originally from South America, chimichurri is a sauce typically made from a variety of minced herbs, oil, and acid, such as vinegar or citrus. Here we use lemon juice, olive oil, and a variety of herbs such as parsley and oregano. Did I happen to mention this all-purpose sauce goes well with everything? I like to keep some on hand in the freezer at all times to quickly brighten up any meal. Double the recipe, freeze some in an ice cube tray, then pop out the cubes and place them in a zip-top plastic bag in the freezer for up to 3 months.

1 In a food processor or blender, add the mint, parsley, olive oil, lemon juice, lemon zest, oregano, garlic, red pepper flakes, and salt. Process until the mixture reaches your desired consistency—anywhere from a slightly chunky to smooth purée. Remove a half cup of the chimichurri mixture and set aside.

2 Pour the remaining chimichurri mixture into a medium bowl or zip-top bag and add the steak. Mix together well and marinate for at least 30 minutes, and up to 8 hours in the refrigerator.

3 In a grill pan over medium-high heat, add the steak and cook 4 minutes on each side (for medium rare). Cook an additional 1 to 2 minutes per side for medium.

4 Place the steak on a cutting board, tent with foil to keep it warm, and let it rest for 10 minutes. Thinly slice the steak crosswise against the grain and serve with the reserved sauce.

COOKING TIP: *Prep the chimichurri sauce the day before, then in the morning place the steak and sauce in a zip-top bag, put it in the refrigerator, and go about your day. When it's dinnertime, you'll have the steak ready to go and cooked in less than 15 minutes!*

Per Serving Calories: 460; Total fat: 38g; Saturated fat: 10g; Cholesterol: 98mg; Sodium: 241mg; Potassium: 505mg; Total Carbohydrates: 5g; Fiber: 2g; Sugars: 1g; Protein: 28g; Magnesium: 45mg; Calcium: 65mg

Lamb Meatballs

SERVES 4 ▪ PREP TIME: 10 MINUTES ▪ COOK TIME: 20 MINUTES

Olive oil cooking spray

1 pound ground lamb

¼ cup fresh mint, chopped

¼ cup shallot, chopped

1 large egg, beaten

1 garlic clove, chopped

1 teaspoon
    ground coriander

1 teaspoon ground cumin

½ teaspoon kosher salt

¼ teaspoon
    ground cinnamon

¼ teaspoon red
    pepper flakes

Fresh mint pairs beautifully with the classic Mediterranean spices cinnamon, cumin, and coriander to liven up these ground lamb meatballs. Once again, I prefer to bake—rather than fry—meatballs to decrease fat, but still maintain a crispy, golden exterior and moist, tender interior. Serve these lamb meatballs with whole-wheat pita and Tzatziki (page 151).

1 Preheat the oven to 400°F. Grease a 12-cup muffin tin with olive oil cooking spray.

2 In a large bowl, combine the lamb, mint, shallot, egg, garlic, coriander, cumin, salt, cinnamon, and red pepper flakes; mix well. Form the mixture into 12 balls and place one in each cup of the prepared muffin tin. Bake for 20 minutes, or until golden brown.

INGREDIENT TIP: *A single portion of lamb provides a variety of essential vitamins and minerals, including iron, vitamin B$_{12}$, niacin, zinc, selenium, and omega-3 fatty acids. Lean lamb is a source of healthy, unsaturated fats, with nearly 40 percent coming from monounsaturated fat.*

SUBSTITUTION TIP: *Ground beef or poultry can be used in place of the lamb, if preferred.*

Per Serving Calories: 350; Total fat: 28g; Saturated fat: 12g; Cholesterol: 129mg; Sodium: 227mg; Potassium: 312mg; Total Carbohydrates: 2g; Fiber: 1g; Sugars: 0g; Protein: 21g; Magnesium: 31mg; Calcium: 42mg

Ground Lamb with Lentils and Pomegranate Seeds

SERVES 4 ▪ PREP TIME: 15 MINUTES ▪ COOK TIME: 15 MINUTES

1 tablespoon extra-virgin olive oil

½ pound ground lamb

1 teaspoon red pepper flakes

½ teaspoon ground cumin

½ teaspoon kosher salt

¼ teaspoon freshly ground black pepper

2 garlic cloves, minced

2 cups cooked, drained lentils

1 hothouse or English cucumber, diced

⅓ cup fresh mint, chopped

⅓ cup fresh parsley, chopped

Zest of 1 lemon

1 cup plain Greek yogurt

½ cup pomegranate seeds

Lamb blends beautifully with crispy lentils, lemony yogurt, and the sweet pop and crunch of pomegranate seeds. To lower the saturated fat in this dish, I decreased the amount of ground lamb but included plenty of plant-based protein from the lentils. To save on prep time, use a 15-ounce can of lentils, drained and rinsed, in this recipe instead of cooking a batch of dried lentils.

1 Heat the olive oil in a large skillet or sauté pan over medium-high heat. Add the lamb and season with the red pepper flakes, cumin, salt, and black pepper. Cook the lamb without stirring until the bottom is brown and crispy, about 5 minutes. Stir and cook for another 5 minutes. Using a spatula, break up the lamb into smaller pieces. Add the garlic and cook, stirring occasionally, for 1 minute. Transfer the lamb mixture to a medium bowl.

2 Add the lentils to the skillet and cook, stirring occasionally, until brown and crisp, about 5 minutes. Return the lamb to the skillet, mix, and warm through, about 3 minutes. Transfer to the large bowl. Add the cucumber, mint, parsley, and lemon zest, mixing together gently.

3 Spoon the yogurt into 4 bowls and top each with some of the lamb mixture. Garnish with the pomegranate seeds.

Per Serving Calories: 370; Total fat: 18g; Saturated fat: 6g; Cholesterol: 44mg; Sodium: 197mg; Potassium: 780mg; Total Carbohydrates: 30g; Fiber: 10g; Sugars: 8g; Protein: 24g; Magnesium: 70mg; Calcium: 110mg

Figs with Mascarpone and
Honey, page 146

Sweets, Sauces, and Staples

Honey Ricotta with Espresso and Chocolate Chips

SERVES 2 ▪ PREP TIME: 5 MINUTES

8 ounces ricotta cheese

2 tablespoons honey

2 tablespoons espresso, chilled or room temperature

1 teaspoon dark chocolate chips or chocolate shavings

Ricotta is extremely versatile and works well in both savory and sweet dishes. For dessert, this honey-sweetened ricotta feels light but tastes rich and decadent. The addition of espresso and chocolate makes this dessert elegant but bold and is sure to satisfy any sweet tooth. Raspberries or diced strawberries are a nice optional addition, as is a splash of liquor, such as amaretto.

1 In a medium bowl, whip together the ricotta cheese and honey until light and smooth, 4 to 5 minutes.

2 Spoon the ricotta cheese–honey mixture evenly into 2 dessert bowls. Drizzle 1 tablespoon espresso into each dish and sprinkle with chocolate chips or shavings.

SUBSTITUTION TIP: *Regular or decaf black coffee can be used in place of the espresso.*

Per Serving Calories: 235; Total fat: 10g; Saturated fat: 6g; Cholesterol: 35mg; Sodium: 115mg; Potassium: 170mg; Total Carbohydrates: 25g; Fiber: 0g; Sugars: 19g; Protein: 13g; Magnesium: 30mg; Calcium: 310mg

Roasted Plums with Nut Crumble

SERVES 4 ■ PREP TIME: 5 MINUTES ■ COOK TIME: 25 MINUTES

¼ cup honey

¼ cup freshly squeezed orange juice

4 large plums, halved and pitted

¼ cup whole-wheat pastry flour

1 tablespoon pure maple sugar

1 tablespoon nuts, coarsely chopped (your choice; I like almonds, pecans, and walnuts)

1½ teaspoons canola oil

½ cup plain Greek yogurt

Stone fruits have a large pit, or "stone," in their center and include plums, peaches, and apricots. They are in season late spring through summer, so look for them at your local farmers' market or grocery store. This recipe works well with any type of stone fruit, but I'm partial to plums. Plums can be found in a wide variety of colors, from yellow to red to dark purple; any will taste great. I love versatility as much as I love plums—and this dish has it. If you're not in the mood for dessert, this dish makes for a luscious brunch dish served over yogurt or steel-cut oats. Getting your daily dose of fruit couldn't be easier or more delicious!

1 Preheat the oven to 400°F. Combine the honey and orange juice in a square baking dish. Place the plums, cut-side down, in the dish. Roast about 15 minutes, and then turn the plums over and roast an additional 10 minutes, or until tender and juicy.

2 In a medium bowl, combine the flour, maple sugar, nuts, and canola oil and mix well. Spread on a small baking sheet and bake alongside the plums, tossing once, until golden brown, about 5 minutes. Set aside until the plums have finished cooking.

3 Serve the plums drizzled with pan juices and topped with the nut crumble and a dollop of yogurt.

Per Serving Calories: 175; Total fat: 3g; Saturated fat: 0g; Cholesterol: 0mg; Sodium: 10mg; Potassium: 215mg; Total Carbohydrates: 36g; Fiber: 2g; Sugars: 28g; Protein: 4g; Magnesium: 22mg; Calcium: 40mg

Figs with Mascarpone and Honey

SERVES 4 ▪ PREP TIME: 5 MINUTES ▪ COOK TIME: 5 MINUTES

1/3 cup walnuts, chopped

8 fresh figs, halved

1/4 cup mascarpone cheese

1 tablespoon honey

1/4 teaspoon flaked sea salt

This dish pulls together many of my favorite foods. As soon as summer hits you'll find me running to the farmers' market for fresh figs. Mascarpone is a rich, velvety, Italian-style cream cheese; adding it with a touch of honey makes these fresh figs that much more luxurious. Serve this for dessert, try it as an appetizer, or make it part of brunch. For an added bit of fun, dish up all the components separately and have your guests make their own!

1 In a skillet over medium heat, toast the walnuts, stirring often, 3 to 5 minutes.

2 Arrange the figs cut-side up on a plate or platter. Using your finger, make a small depression in the cut side of each fig and fill with mascarpone cheese. Sprinkle with a bit of the walnuts, drizzle with the honey, and add a tiny pinch of sea salt.

Per Serving Calories: 200; Total fat: 13g; Saturated fat: 4g; Cholesterol: 18mg; Sodium: 105mg; Potassium: 230mg; Total Carbohydrates: 24g; Fiber: 3g; Sugars: 18g; Protein: 3g; Magnesium: 30mg; Calcium: 53mg

Greek Yogurt Chocolate "Mousse" with Berries

SERVES 4 ▪ PREP TIME: 15 MINUTES, PLUS 15 MINUTES TO CHILL

2 cups plain Greek yogurt

¼ cup heavy cream

¼ cup pure maple syrup

3 tablespoons unsweetened cocoa powder

2 teaspoons vanilla extract

¼ teaspoon kosher salt

1 cup fresh mixed berries

¼ cup chocolate chips

This tangy yogurt "mousse" is quicker, simpler, and healthier than the conventional recipe, without sacrificing any taste or texture. If you don't have any chocolate chips, use chocolate shavings. I like to use whole blueberries and raspberries with this recipe, but diced strawberries also pair beautifully.

1 Place the yogurt, cream, maple syrup, cocoa powder, vanilla, and salt in the bowl of a stand mixer or use a large bowl with an electric hand mixer. Mix at medium-high speed until fluffy, about 5 minutes.

2 Spoon evenly among 4 bowls and put in the refrigerator to set for at least 15 minutes.

3 Serve each bowl with ¼ cup mixed berries and 1 tablespoon chocolate chips.

Per Serving Calories: 300; Total fat: 11g; Saturated fat: 6g; Cholesterol: 27mg; Sodium: 60mg; Potassium: 295mg; Total Carbohydrates: 35g; Fiber: 3g; Sugars: 29g; Protein: 16g; Magnesium: 25mg; Calcium: 190mg

Individual Meringues with Strawberries, Mint, and Toasted Coconut

SERVES 6 ▪ PREP TIME: 25 MINUTES ▪ COOK TIME: 1 HOUR, 30 MINUTES

4 large egg whites

1 teaspoon vanilla extract

½ teaspoon cream of tartar

¾ cup sugar

8 ounces strawberries, diced

¼ cup fresh mint, chopped

¼ cup unsweetened shredded coconut, toasted

I love meringue—it's crisp, soft, gooey, and just delicious. To up the nutrient density, I decreased the amount of sugar used and added flavor, texture, and depth with fruit, herbs, and coconut. If you'd like to make this a little more decadent, add a dollop of whipped cream or mascarpone cheese.

1 Preheat the oven to 225°F. Line 2 baking sheets with parchment paper.

2 Place the egg whites, vanilla, and cream of tartar in the bowl of a stand mixer (or use a large bowl with an electric hand mixer); beat at medium speed until soft peaks form, about 2 to 3 minutes. Increase to high speed and gradually add the sugar, beating until stiff peaks form and the mixture looks shiny and smooth, about 2 to 3 minutes.

3 Using a spatula or spoon, drop ⅓ cup of meringue onto a prepared baking sheet; smooth out and make shapelier as desired. In total, make 12 dollops, 6 per sheet, leaving at least 1 inch between dollops.

4 Bake for 1½ hours, rotating baking sheets between top and bottom, front and back, halfway through. After 1½ hours, turn off the oven, but keep the door closed. Leave the meringues in the oven for an additional 30 minutes. You can leave the meringues in the oven even longer (or overnight), or you may let them finish cooling to room temperature.

5 Combine the strawberries, mint, and coconut in a medium bowl. Serve 2 meringues per person topped with the fruit mixture.

COOKING TIP: *Crisp, dry meringue will keep for several weeks at room temperature in airtight containers; do not refrigerate or freeze. Add toppings when you are ready to serve.*

SUBSTITUTION TIP: *Don't like coconut? Sliced almonds are a great substitute, or try any other nuts that you like.*

Per Serving Calories: 150; Total fat: 2g; Saturated fat: 2g; Cholesterol: 0mg; Sodium: 40mg; Potassium: 165mg; Total Carbohydrates: 29g; Fiber: 1g; Sugars: 27g; Protein: 3g; Magnesium: 11mg; Calcium: 11mg

Pistachio-Stuffed Dates

SERVES 4 ▪ PREP TIME: 10 MINUTES

½ cup unsalted pistachios, shelled

¼ teaspoon kosher salt

8 Medjool dates, pitted

Medjool dates taste so decadent and sweet that they could pass for candy. Paired with salty, earthy pistachio nut butter, you get a dessert or snack that hits the sweet (and salty) spot. You can swap out the pistachios for other nuts or use a jar of any chunky-style nut butter you like instead of making your own.

1 In a food processor, add the pistachios and salt. Process until combined to a chunky nut butter, 3 to 5 minutes.

2 Split open the dates and spoon the pistachio nut butter into each half.

Per Serving Calories: 220; Total fat: 7g; Saturated fat: 1g; Cholesterol: 0mg; Sodium: 70mg; Potassium: 490mg; Total Carbohydrates: 41g; Fiber: 5g; Sugars: 33g; Protein: 4g; Magnesium: 43mg; Calcium: 47mg

Tzatziki

MAKES 1½ CUPS ▪ PREP TIME: 10 MINUTES

2 Persian cucumbers or ½ hothouse or English cucumber

1 cup plain Greek yogurt

2 tablespoons fresh dill, chopped

2 tablespoons fresh mint, chopped

2 tablespoons lemon juice

1 tablespoon extra-virgin olive oil

1 garlic clove, minced

½ teaspoon kosher salt

I love tzatziki. Refreshing cucumber, creamy Greek yogurt, and zingy lemon make it the perfect dipping sauce and accompaniment for just about everything. It's one of those things I like to whip up every few days and keep on hand. It goes well with so many different dishes, including the Greek Turkey Burger (page 127) and Za'atar Chicken Tenders (page 132). When you grate the cucumbers, use the large holes for a chunkier version or the small holes for a smoother version.

1 Using a box grater, grate the cucumbers.

2 In a medium bowl, combine the grated cucumbers, yogurt, dill, mint, lemon juice, olive oil, garlic, and salt; mix well.

COOKING TIP: *Tzatziki should stay fresh in the refrigerator up to 5 days. Just give it a good stir before serving.*

Per Serving (¼ cup) Calories: 45; Total fat: 0g; Saturated fat: 0g; Cholesterol: 0mg; Sodium: 105mg; Potassium: 125mg; Total Carbohydrates: 3g; Fiber: 0g; Sugars: 2g; Protein: 3g; Magnesium: 10mg; Calcium: 45mg

Salsa Verde

MAKES 1 CUP ▪ PREP TIME: 5 MINUTES

2 cups parsley

¼ cup lemon juice

2 teaspoons capers, rinsed

4 anchovies, chopped

½ teaspoon kosher salt

¼ teaspoon freshly ground black pepper

½ cup extra-virgin olive oil

This herby relish can vary by region in Italy. Its base of parsley and oil is generally the same as in other versions, but capers inject a sharp briny bite, while lemon juice balances the overall flavor. Use this sauce to add flavor to a variety of foods, including grains, meat, poultry, and fish. Serve it with the Crispy Mediterranean Chicken Thighs (page 126) or mix it into the Italian White Bean Salad with Bell Peppers (page 73).

Add the parsley, lemon juice, capers, anchovies, salt, and black pepper to a food processor. Process until minced. Add the olive oil and process until it reaches your desired consistency. Refrigerate until ready to use. Any leftovers can be stored in an airtight container for up to 1 week.

SUBSTITUTION TIP: *1 tablespoon of anchovy paste can be used in place of the anchovies.*

Per Serving (2 tablespoons) Calories: 130; Total fat: 14g; Saturated fat: 2g; Cholesterol: 1mg; Sodium: 160mg; Potassium: 95mg; Total Carbohydrates: 2g; Fiber: 1g; Sugars: 0g; Protein: 1g; Magnesium: 8mg; Calcium: 22mg

Lemon Tahini Dressing

MAKES ½ CUP • PREP TIME: 5 MINUTES

1/4 cup tahini

3 tablespoons lemon juice

3 tablespoons warm water

1/4 teaspoon kosher salt

1/4 teaspoon pure
maple syrup

1/4 teaspoon ground cumin

1/8 teaspoon cayenne pepper

Great dressings are easy to make and provide depth and flavor to a dish. Tahini is sesame seed paste, full of flavor and nutrients, including fiber, plant-based protein, and iron. Here's a bonus fact—the vitamin C from the lemon juice helps with absorbing the plant-based iron found in the tahini. This dressing is a delicious addition to vegetables, poultry, meat, and fish, as well as a straight-up dipping sauce for pita bread.

In a medium bowl, whisk together the tahini, lemon juice, water, salt, maple syrup, cumin, and cayenne pepper until smooth. Place in the refrigerator until ready to serve. Store any leftovers in the refrigerator in an airtight container up to 5 days.

Per Serving (2 tablespoons) Calories: 90; Total fat: 7g; Saturated fat: 1g; Cholesterol: 0mg; Sodium: 80mg; Potassium: 77mg; Total Carbohydrates: 5g; Fiber: 1g; Sugars: 1g; Protein: 3g; Magnesium: 15mg; Calcium: 66mg

Yogurt Tahini Dressing

MAKES 1 CUP ▪ PREP TIME: 5 MINUTES

- ½ cup plain Greek yogurt
- ⅓ cup tahini
- ¼ cup freshly squeezed orange juice
- ½ teaspoon kosher salt

Combining yogurt, tahini, and orange juice creates a very delicious—and addictive—dressing. It is a terrific complement to Beef Kofta (page 137) or Yogurt-Marinated Chicken Kebabs (page 136) and a good dip for raw vegetables and pita bread. Add ground cumin or coriander for a spicier variation. This is definitely a crowd-pleaser no matter what!

In a medium bowl, whisk together the yogurt, tahini, orange juice, and salt until smooth. Place in the refrigerator until ready to serve. Store leftovers in an airtight container in the refrigerator for up to 5 days.

Per Serving (2 tablespoons) Calories: 70; Total fat: 2g; Saturated fat: 1g; Cholesterol: 0mg; Sodium: 80mg; Potassium: 85mg; Total Carbohydrates: 4g; Fiber: 1g; Sugars: 1g; Protein: 4g; Magnesium: 12mg; Calcium: 66mg

Lemon Vinaigrette

MAKES 1 CUP ▪ PREP TIME: 5 MINUTES

¼ cup lemon juice

¼ cup white wine vinegar

2 tablespoons
    shallot, minced

2 teaspoons Dijon mustard

½ teaspoon honey

½ teaspoon kosher salt

¼ teaspoon freshly ground
    black pepper

½ cup extra-virgin olive oil

Vinaigrette dressings are an essential part of my kitchen. I like to keep some sort of vinaigrette on hand at all times. Full of flavor and color, this versatile vinaigrette is great as a dressing or marinade. The lemon juice brightens while the oil adds richness, lending a refreshing flavor to all types of foods.

In a medium bowl, whisk together the lemon juice, vinegar, shallot, mustard, honey, salt, and black pepper. Add the olive oil and whisk well. Store any leftovers in the refrigerator in an airtight container for up to 5 days.

SUBSTITUTION TIP: *Apple cider vinegar, champagne vinegar, or sherry vinegar will go nicely in place of the white wine vinegar.*

Per Serving (2 tablespoons) Calories: 125; Total fat: 14g; Saturated fat: 2g; Cholesterol: 0mg; Sodium: 100mg; Potassium: 17mg; Total Carbohydrates: 1g; Fiber: 0g; Sugars: 1g; Protein: 0g; Magnesium: 1mg; Calcium: 1mg

Olive Mint Vinaigrette

MAKES ½ CUP ▪ PREP TIME: 5 MINUTES

¼ cup white wine vinegar

¼ teaspoon honey

¼ teaspoon kosher salt

¼ teaspoon freshly ground black pepper

¼ cup extra-virgin olive oil

¼ cup olives, pitted and minced

2 tablespoons fresh mint, minced

This vinaigrette goes particularly well with fish, meat, and poultry. The combination of salty, briny olives with fresh mint gives foods an extra something special. I like to use this as a marinade for chicken or fish, mixed into warm whole grains, tossed with roasted vegetables, or as a dressing for a simple green salad.

In a bowl, whisk together the vinegar, honey, salt, and black pepper. Add the olive oil and whisk well. Add the olives and mint, and mix well. Store any leftovers in the refrigerator in an airtight container for up to 5 days.

Per Serving (2 tablespoons) Calories: 135; Total fat: 15g; Saturated fat: 2g; Cholesterol: 0mg; Sodium: 135mg; Potassium: 6mg; Total Carbohydrates: 1g; Fiber: 0g; Sugars: 0g; Protein: 0g; Magnesium: 1mg; Calcium: 2mg

Measurement Conversions

VOLUME EQUIVALENTS (LIQUID)

US STANDARD	US STANDARD (OUNCES)	METRIC (APPROXIMATE)
2 tablespoons	1 fl. oz.	30 mL
¼ cup	2 fl. oz.	60 mL
½ cup	4 fl. oz.	120 mL
1 cup	8 fl. oz.	240 mL
1½ cups	12 fl. oz.	355 mL
2 cups or 1 pint	16 fl. oz.	475 mL
4 cups or 1 quart	32 fl. oz.	1 L
1 gallon	128 fl. oz.	4 L

OVEN TEMPERATURES

FAHRENHEIT (F)	CELSIUS (C) (APPROXIMATE)
250°	120°
300°	150°
325°	165°
350°	180°
375°	190°
400°	200°
425°	220°
450°	230°

VOLUME EQUIVALENTS (DRY)

US STANDARD	METRIC (APPROXIMATE)
⅛ teaspoon	0.5 mL
¼ teaspoon	1 mL
½ teaspoon	2 mL
¾ teaspoon	4 mL
1 teaspoon	5 mL
1 tablespoon	15 mL
¼ cup	59 mL
⅓ cup	79 mL
½ cup	118 mL
⅔ cup	156 mL
¾ cup	177 mL
1 cup	235 mL
2 cups or 1 pint	475 mL
3 cups	700 mL
4 cups or 1 quart	1 L

WEIGHT EQUIVALENTS

US STANDARD	METRIC (APPROXIMATE)
½ ounce	15 g
1 ounce	30 g
2 ounces	60 g
4 ounces	115 g
8 ounces	225 g
12 ounces	340 g
16 ounces or 1 pound	455 g

References

Ahmad, Shafqat, M. Vinayaga Moorthy, Olga V. Demler, et al. "Assessment of Risk Factors and Biomarkers Associated with Risk of Cardiovascular Disease among Women Consuming a Mediterranean Diet." *JAMA Network Open* 1, no. 8 (December 2018). doi:10.1001/jamanetworkopen.2018.5708.

Albuquerque, Rita CR, Valéria Baltar, and Dirce M. L. Marchioni. "Breast Cancer and Dietary Patterns: A Systematic Review." *Nutrition Reviews* 72, no. 1 (December 2013): 1–17. doi:10.1111/nure.12083.

Fung, Teresa T., Kathryn M. Rexrode, Christos S. Mantzoros, et al. "Mediterranean Diet and Incidence of and Mortality from Coronary Heart Disease and Stroke in Women." *Circulation* 119, no. 8 (March 2009): 1093–100. https://doi.org/10.1161/CIRCULATIONAHA.108.816736.

Giugliano, Dario, Antonio Ceriello, and Katherine Esposito. "The Effects of Diet on Inflammation: Emphasis on the Metabolic Syndrome." *Journal of the American College of Cardiology* 48, no. 4 (August 2006): 677–85. doi:10.1016/j.jacc.2006.03/052.

Lopez-Garcia, Esther, Fernando Rodriguez-Artalejo, Tricia Y. Li, et al. "The Mediterranean-Style Dietary Pattern and Mortality among Men and Women with Cardiovascular Disease." *American Journal of Clinical Nutrition* 99, no. 1 (January 2014): 172–80. doi:10.3945/ajcn.113.068106.

Mamalaki, Eirini, Costas Anastasiou, Mary Kosmidis, et al. "Associations between the Mediterranean Diet and Sleep in the Elderly."

Clinical Nutrition ESPEN 24 (April 2018): 185. https://doi
.org/10.1016/j.clnesp.2018.01.051.

Mancini, Joseph G., Kristian B. Filion, Renée Atallah, et al. "Systematic Review of the Mediterranean Diet for Long-Term Weight Loss." *American Journal of Medicine* 129, no. 4 (April 2016): 407–15. https://doi.org/10.1016/j.amjmed.2015.11.028.

Mena-Sánchez, Guillermo, Nancy Babio, Miguel Á. Martínez-González, et al. "Fermented Dairy Products, Diet Quality, and Cardio–Metabolic Profile of a Mediterranean Cohort at High Cardiovascular Risk." *Nutrition, Metabolism and Cardiovascular Diseases* 28, no. 10 (October 2018): 1002–11. https://doi.org/10.1016/j.numecd.2018.05.006.

Nielsen, Samara Joy, Maria Angélica Trak-Fellermeier, and Kaumudi Joshipura. "The Association between Dietary Fiber Intake and CRP Levels, US Adults, 2007–2010." Supplement, *FASEB Journal* 31, no. S1 (April 2017).

Salas-Salvadó, Jordi, Mónica Bulló, Nancy Babio, et al. "Reduction in the Incidence of Type 2 Diabetes with the Mediterranean Diet." *Diabetes Care* 34, no. 1 (October 2010): 14–19. doi:10.2337/dc10-1288.

Schwingshackl, Lukas, and Georg Hoffmann. "Adherence to Mediterranean Diet and Risk of Cancer: An Updated Systematic Review and Meta-Analysis of Observational Studies." *Cancer Medicine* 4, no. 12 (October 2015): 1933–47. doi:10.1002/cam4.539.

Tapsell, Linda C. "Fermented Dairy Food and CVD Risk." Supplement, *British Journal of Nutrition* 113, no. S2 (April 2015): S131-35. doi:10.1017/S0007114514002359.

Yu, Zhi, Vasanti Malik, NaNa Keum, et al. "Associations between Nut Consumption and Inflammatory Biomarkers." *American Journal of Clinical Nutrition* 104, no. 3 (September 2016): 722–28. doi:10.3945/ajcn.116.134205.

Index

Acknowledgments

Thanks to my parents, who are such terrible cooks that it sparked my interest in food and the desire to learn how to cook, compelling me to seek out culinary training and igniting my passion for creating healthy, delicious food.

Thanks to TJO for tasting an endless array of different foods, willingness to take care of the dishes, continued support in life, and teaching me that watching golf can be relaxing—especially after a day spent cooking and writing.

Thanks to all my amazing friends who helped with testing, tasting, brainstorming, reading, editing, and ongoing support during the care and feeding of this book . . . and life in general.

Thanks to my interns extraordinaire: Mary, who helped with brainstorming, developing, testing, tasting, and countless hours of prepping, chopping, and cooking; and Lexi, who held down the fort while I was working on this labor of love.

Thanks to my colleagues and friends, who are a constant inspiration and support network.

Thanks to the Callisto publishing team and to photographer Moya McAllister for supporting me through this journey.

Thanks to all of you who have picked up this book and taken it into the kitchen—cooking, trying new things, and getting your hands dirty. I hope you find favorites, dog-ear some pages, and get oil stains on others.

About the Author

 **ABBIE GELLMAN, MS, RD, CDN** is a chef and registered dietitian with a master's degree in nutrition education. She is the founder of Culinary Nutrition Cuisine, where she is a culinary nutrition consultant, spokesperson, recipe developer, product developer, educator, culinary nutrition media expert—and now cookbook author. Abbie is a member of the Science Advisory Board for Jenny Craig, providing ongoing cutting-edge counsel to update the education and lifestyle strategies of the company. She is regularly featured in the media, where she shares culinary expertise and delicious, nutritious recipes. Abbie also hosts cooking and nutrition videos which can be found on her website, CulinaryNutritionCuisine.com, YouTube Channel, @CulinaryNutritionCuisine, and other social media platforms.

Printed in the USA
CPSIA information can be obtained
at www.ICGtesting.com
CBHW040225120324
5243CB00002B/9